Edible Wild Plants:

Over 111 Natural Foods and Over 22 Plant-Based Recipes On A Budget

Joseph Erickson

© Copyright 2020 by Joseph Erickson. All right reserved.

The work contained herein has been produced with the intent to provide relevant knowledge and information on the topic on the topic described in the title for entertainment purposes only. While the author has gone to every extent to furnish up to date and true information, no claims can be made as to its accuracy or validity as the author has made no claims to be an expert on this topic. Notwithstanding, the reader is asked to do their own research and consult any subject matter experts they deem necessary to ensure the quality and accuracy of the material presented herein.

This statement is legally binding as deemed by the Committee of Publishers Association and the American Bar Association for the territory of the United States. Other jurisdictions may apply their own legal statutes. Any reproduction, transmission, or copying of this material contained in this work without the express written consent of the copyright holder shall be deemed as a copyright violation as per the current legislation in force on the date of publishing and subsequent time thereafter. All additional works derived from this material may be claimed by the holder of this copyright.

The data, depictions, events, descriptions, and all other information forthwith are considered to be true, fair, and accurate unless the work is expressly described as a work of fiction. Regardless of the nature of this work, the Publisher is exempt from any responsibility of actions taken by the reader in conjunction with this work. The Publisher acknowledges that the reader acts of their own accord and releases the author and Publisher of any responsibility for the observance of tips, advice, counsel, strategies and techniques that may be offered in this volume.

TABLE OF CONTENTS

INTRODUCTION 1

CHAPTER 1 *HISTORY OF HERBALISM* 3

    ARABS SAVE THE GREEK SCIENCES 6

    BYZANTINE EMPIRE 8

    ANCIENT GREEK MEDICINE 10

    EARLY MIDDLE AGE EUROPEAN MEDICINE 12

    ARAB INFLUENCES 15

    BAGHDAD 17

    QUICK REVIEW 20

    CENTRAL ASIA AVICENNA 21

    REAWAKENING OF EUROPE 24

CHAPTER 2 *KNOWING YOUR ENVIRONMENT* 27

    FOREST LAND 28

    CONIFEROUS FOREST 29

    MEDITERRANEAN 30

    GRASSLANDS 31

    TUNDRA 32

    ALPINE 32

    RAINFOREST 33

    DESERT 33

    EDIBLE PLANTS IN NORTHEAST US 35

    EDIBLE PLANTS IN SOUTHWEST US 39

    EDIBLE PLANTS IN SOUTHEAST US 42

    EDIBLE PLANTS IN NORTHWEST US 43

    Edible Plants in Midwest US 45

    Edible Plants in South Central US 46

CHAPTER 3 *COMPENDIUM OF EDIBLE PLANTS* 48

CHAPTER 4 *COMPENDIUM OF MEDICINAL PLANTS* 86

CHAPTER 5 *COMPENDIUM OF POISONOUS PLANTS* 95

CHAPTER 6 *THE BASICS OF FORAGING* 103

    Make Sure You Can Be on the Land 104

    Know How to Identify Plants and Forage Safely 104

    Remember the Four Rs 105

    Know Your Protect Species 105

    Don't Take the Only Plant 106

    Take Only What You Need 106

    Harvest Your Plants Wisely 106

CHAPTER 7 *RECIPES FOR EDIBLE WILD PLANTS* 108

    Buffalo Milkweed Pods 108

    Cattail Rice 110

    Dandy Pasta 111

    Garlic Mustard Stuffed Mushrooms 112

    Kale, Lambs Quarters, and Cheese Manicotti 113

    Purslane Egg Cups 115

    Stuffed Milkweed Pods 116

    Weed Burgers 117

    Wild Potato Pancakes 118

    Wild Roasted Cabbage 120

    Buttered Chickweed 122

    Plantain Salad 123

Blueberry Labrador Tea *124*

Burdock Tonic Tea *125*

Healthy Heart Tea *126*

Highbush Cranberry Juice *127*

Immune Boosting Coffee *128*

Fennel and Angelica Cookies *129*

Bee Balm Cookies *130*

Coltsfoot Sorbet *131*

Dandelion Banana Bread *132*

Honey Cattail Cookies *133*

Nutty Plantain Snack *134*

Pine Cookies *135*

Pine Rum Balls *136*

CONCLUSION **137**

INTRODUCTION

First off, I would like to thank you for choosing this book. I hope that you find it informative and helpful in whatever your goals may be. Throughout this book, we are going to talk about the different aspects of foraging, herbalism, and edible wild plants so that you can enjoy the benefits of eating food in its most natural form.

The world is full of plants. In each area of the world, the plants have adapted to survive their environment, and as such, they have learned how to handle the wildlife of that area. In some cases, this includes humans. While the people in New York may not have the same types of wild plants available to them as people in Texas do, they still have a lot of tasty and healthy options to forage for.

You may be wondering why we are talking about foraging for plants when there are grocery stores on every corner. Well, there may come a time when we can't fully rely on our modern infrastructure to provide users with the necessities we need, especially when it comes to food. But it's not only that. The food you buy in the grocery store has been on the shelves for who knows how long. The produce was picked long before it was fully ripe so that it could travel hundreds of miles without spoiling. While the produce still has important nutrients and minerals in them, they aren't at the same concentration they would be if you picked it off of the tree yourself.

Do you see where I'm going with this?

Moreover, wild plants have medicinal applications and can help with pest control. So not only can you go into your backyard and grab some dandelion greens for dinner, but you also may be able to find some Echinacea to help with your cold. If you got some mint to harvest, you can use that to help keep some pests at bay as well.

You see, nature provides us with an endless supply of possibilities. If you would like to have control over the food you eat, then learning how to forage for food is a great way to do so.

This book will help to guide you through this process. We will go over what herbalism is and what role it played in the history of man. Then we will look at learning more about your environment so that you know what types of foods you can find. We'll also cover the basics of ethical foraging so that you never harm the environment when you go looking for foods. You will also find lists of edible and medicinal plants and how to use them. Of course, you will also find a list of poisonous plants so that you don't end up hurting yourself. Lastly, you'll find some delicious recipes that you can make using your freshly harvested wild plants.

Learning how to forage is a rewarding experience, and I hope you have fun on your first trip out.

Before we get started, I would like to ask that if you find any part of this book helpful or informative, please leave a review.

CHAPTER 1

History Of Herbalism

Using plants for medicinal purposes has been around since ancient Babylonians, Egyptians, Indians, Chinese, and Native Americans. All of these cultures were herbalists. The oldest list of medicinal herbs was called *Shennong Ben Cao Jing* or *Shen Nung Pen Ts'ao,* which is a book about medicinal plants and agriculture. This text is thought to be a compilation of every oral tradition that was written between 200 and 250 CE. It has been said that this text was made from three volumes that contained 365 entries on medicinal plants and a description of each.

The ancient Romans and Greeks were also great herbalists. Surgeons that traveled with the Roman army took their expertise about herbs and spread it through the Roman Empire. They took it into England, France, Germany, and Spain. Galen and Dioscorides, who were surgeons from Greece that traveled with the Roman army, compiled a list of herbs that became the definitive materials for their medical text for about 1500 years.

During the Middle Ages, the monasteries of mainland Europe and Britain preserved herbalism. Before universities were established during the 11th and 12th centuries, monasteries were used as medical schools. Monks would translate and copy the works of Galen, Dioscorides, and Hippocrates. Their gardens were growing the most useful and common herbs that served as training grounds for the following generations of laymen, monks, and physicians.

Because of the Islamic conquest in North Africa during the 7th and 8th centuries, Arabic scholars were able to attain a lot of Roman and Greek texts. The Iranian physician Ibn Sina who was also known as Avicenna, combined the traditions of Galen and Dioscorides with his own ancient practices in a text called *The Canon of Medicine*. It was the most influential text that was ever written. It spread throughout Europe during the 11th and 12th centuries.

Due to the printing press being invented in the middle of the 15th century, the texts of Avicenna, Galen, and Dioscorides were mass-produced and were accessible by people who lived outside of the palace, the university, and the monastery. Using herbs didn't require any special skills. The readers just had to gather their herbs and apply them as described in the text.

Every herbalist who found a new use for an herb tried to standardize the use of this plant. One person who sought to do this was Theophrastus Bombastus von Hohenheim, who was also known as Paracelsus. He emphasized how important it was to get to know a patient rather than just blindly using herbs as a cure.

In spite of his distrust of herbalism, she revived the "doctrine of signatures." According to this, each herb had a particular "sign." Which was how the plant looked, its living environment, scent, or color would show how it was to be used. Any herb that was used to cure jaundice would include dandelions, marigolds, or other plants that had yellow-colored flowers. Pansies that have heart-shaped petals would be used to help heart problems.

One hundred years later, Nicholas Culpeper, an Englishman, brought back another facet of ancient herbalism, and this was astrology. These kinds of herbalists would connect an herb to various signs of the zodiac. They would treat certain ailments by figuring out what planet and sign ruled over a specific body part that needed to be cared for and would then prescribe an herb that had the same astrological sign. Culpeper stated: "he that would know the reason for the operation of the herbs, must look up as high as the stars."

Even though Culpeper and Paracelsus promoted astrological herbalism and the doctrine of signatures, the practice of medicine was changing. Men such as William Harvey and

Francis Bacon were transforming science from being speculative into an experimental process. This didn't mix well with astrology and doctrine of signatures, and so medical and biological science started separating from herbalism. The herbalists who focused on classification wouldn't acknowledge the stars and signatures that eventually formed botany. The doctors who found Harvey's circulation of blood more useful than the planet's movements began what could have been called scientific medicine.

These four herbalists highlighted here were the forerunners of herbal medicine from its beginning to when it changed into medical science.

Arabs Save the Greek Sciences

In the past ten years or so, I have become interested in herbal medicine's history, and I decided to read some of the authors of the day, but I focused on Western European, East Indian, Arab, Greek, and Egyptian. I found a colorful and rich array of cultures, societies, religions, wars, circumstances, and characters that began the medical and herbal traditions that we know today.

The study of herbal, botanical, and medical history was motivated by what I had heard in different herbal and medicine classes and had read in texts about these fields. What upset me the most was that most of the time, these "tales" were spread without even thinking about whether or not they were true. A colleague of mine stated: "herbal legends are rampant in our field."

Without an accurate description of religious beliefs, societal conditions, cultural morays, interactions of cultures, discoveries, events, and so on, we could fall prey to what has been agreed upon, and most of the time misquoted statements about our herbal traditions. Most people just live with these ideas and believe these false conceptions.

If we don't know the roots that herbalism came from, we will just create a myth or story that favors a certain belief about our scenes, views, or the lives we are part of. You could say: "Women have always been suppressed; just look at the way women who were herbalists were killed. This is why we lost our knowledge." Another interesting belief that has been spread around is: "This healing method was given to this tribe and is the oldest form of medicine, and this is the end of it." These statements limit our views, and they normally aren't true and could lead to a rigid philosophic view. Most of the time, these ideas that have been misconstrued are defended with a lot of arrogance, and the people who think like this are not open to discussing anything else.

If we can put these things in a bigger historic picture, it will open us up to be able to look at this healing art in various ways. We won't get trapped in a certain way of thinking. We will continue to be amazed at how determined humans have been and the curiosity that can't be satisfied, along with our ability to forget all the things we have achieved so far.

It's hard to figure out how to start this as this subject is just so large. With all the cultures beginning, ending, and then melding into another culture, wars, religious wars, a culture's forgetfulness, finding the information again, all the superstitions, how the world looks at this, and on and on and on.

Another problem that is encountered when describing this topic is that there are certain areas in history where people have experienced different views. Our experiences today as modern American's are very different from a Syrian refugee's experience. Speaking historically, I have heard people make statements such as: "During the Dark Ages learning about medicine was stagnant." You have to first know what period of time we were talking about, and what part of the world you are talking about. During 600 AD, superstitions ran rampant during Western Europe, but there were a lot of expansions and learning about herbal and medical knowledge within the Byzantine Empire.

I'll begin this historical journey when the Western Roman Empire collapsed during the fifth century. During this period, and for 500 years more, Western Europe had lost a connection with most of its heritage. All that remained of the Greek sciences were Pliny's *Encyclopedia* and Boethius's texts on mathematics and logic. Pliny ended up dying in Pompeii because he was curious about what happened with a volcano erupted. When he made his trip there, he died from the fumes of the eruption. They had such a limited library that theologians found it pretty much impossible to learn more.

Byzantine Empire

In 395 AD, the Roman Empire had been split into West and East because of theological differences. After the fall of the Western Empire, the Eastern Empire decided to claim the Roman world. The boundaries of Rome were shifted, and the Byzantine Empire was centered on the Southern Balkan Peninsula and Asia Minor. During the 1000 years that it existed, the empire was constantly upset by internal political and religious strife and invaders. In spite of this complex administration, moral decay, and gross violence, the empire continued with the Greco-Roman civilization and blended it with the Middle Eastern influences. All this was happening while the West was in complete chaos. During all the years of divisions, wars, turmoil, and being encompassed by the Ottoman Turks, Constantinople fell to Muhammad II in 1453. This began the shit to the modern era. The Byzantine Empire was mainly Green in nature since they spoke Greek, and their main religion was Christian Orthodoxy.

Even though all the turmoil, the medicine of the Byzantine was practiced from 400 AD to 1453 AD. For about 500 years, the herbal and medicinal roots of Western Europe stagnated by superstitions, but within the Eastern Roman Empire, herbal medicine was still going strong. They drew knowledge from Ancient Roman and Greek books that have been preserved in its large library. But medicine continued to be one of the few sciences that the Byzantines were better at than their Greco-Roman predecessors. Because of this, we are able to see the way their medicine influenced Arabic medicine, as well as Western medicine's rebirth during the Renaissance. Anytime the word medicine is used, it will be referring to all kinds of herbs.

The physicians in Byzantine would compile all their knowledge into books. They would elaborately decorate these books with illustrations showing a certain ailment. Paul of Aegina wrote *The Medical Compendium in Seven Books*. This book was written during the late 7th century AD. It stayed in used as a textbook for over 800 years.

There was a revolution in medicine, and there are several sources that mention hospitals being established. Constantinople was probably the center of all of this during the Middle Ages due to all of their knowledge, their geographical location, and their wealth.

Ancient Greek Medicine

This will be a very brief overview. There isn't time or space to tell you everything about this era of medicine.

Byzantium and Western Europe medicine were created by the Ancient Greeks medicine, and this was influenced by Egyptian and Babylonian traditions. Hippocrates, a Greek physician, created humoral medicine that was made up of four humors, phlegm, black bile, yellow bile, and blood. He used the elements in the nature of air, fire, water, and earth to get these back into balance.

Hippocrates has been called the "father of modern medicine." There are around 70 medical works that were created from Hippocrates and his students. This collection is known as The Hippocratic Corpus. He also came up with the Hippocratic Oath that physicians still take today.

Hippocrates and his followers were the first to start describing many different medical conditions and diseases. He had gotten credit for his critical thinking within the medical world, and for finding the cause of disease through logic and observation. He did his best to get rid of superstitions and metaphysical causes of diseases. He found these ideas to not be effective, and they didn't help relieve the conditions of his patients.

The next authority on plant-based medicine was Pandonios Dioscorides in both Western Europe and Eastern Arab Empire. Dioscorides tried to come up with a good field guide that contained plants that can be helpful in medicine. He wanted to discover a way to retrieve that kind of information that he needed in order to treat people. Dioscorides was one of the first people to say: "Anyone wanting experience in these matters must encounter the plants as shoots newly emerged from the earth, plants in their prime, and plants in their decline. For someone who has come across the shoot alone cannot know the mature plant, nor if he has seen only the opened plants can he recognize the young shoot as well." He gained information from traditions and knowledge and mentioned others like Theophrastus. Theophrastus had tried to learn about all plant families. He believed plant superstitions should not be used and tried to place plants into categories that had some sort of order. This information was split between five books:

- Sharp aromatic herbs
- Pot herbs
- Cereals
- Shrubs and trees that produce raw materials that can be used medically
- Resinous and oily plants that can be used to make aromatic ointments and salves

He also talks about how important juices and roots of the plants are, too. He has listed the seeds that can be used medicinally and created an inventory of all the cordials and wines that he used to treat his patients.

Later in Rome, Galen, another Greek physician, was a great surgeon during the ancient world and performed various surgeries, which included eye and brain operations that nobody tried again for nearly 2000 years. He wrote more about herbs and was able to identify herbs that grow in various locations. He also created another version of the humoral system of medicine that was more rigid but did contribute to more inquiry about surgery, wound healing, and herbal medicine.

Early Middle Age European Medicine

During the 5th and 9th centuries in Europe, all their medical knowledge came from the surviving Roman and Greek texts that had been preserved mostly in monasteries. All the ideas about the cure and origin of diseases weren't completely religious but had been based on a spiritual view where factors like the will of the gods, curses, possessions, demons, astral influences, sin, and destiny took more precedence than the physical cause. One author called this "social consensus" and "shamanistic complex." The effectiveness of these cures was based on their belief in the doctor and patient instead of based on empirical evidence. The new view became centered in the Church that forced their influences on medicine.

The center of the new view became the Church that forced their influences on medicine. Since Christianity emphasized compassion and cared for the sick, monks ran the hospitals, but they didn't function like hospitals do today. These were areas where people who were seriously sick were taken. These people were either expected to get better or die according to God's will. There weren't many physicians to tend to these people, just kind monks who gave these people comfort, various herbal medicines, and the sacraments of healing.

Since the Church looked at caring for the soul as more important than caring for our bodies, physical cleanliness and medical treatments were not valued. Being able to deny all bodily desires was viewed as being saintly. With time, almost all Western Europeans looked at illnesses as any condition that was created through a supernatural factor that could end up becoming a diabolical possession. Because of this, cures were only able to be given through religious means. During this time, the Church had a lot of influence on every aspect of people's lives.

Every malady would have a patron saint that prayers were said to that was sent up by the community, friends, family, and patient. Upper respiratory infections could be prevented through blessing the person's throat with candles that had been crossed on the feast of Saint Blaise. Saint Roch was the patron saint of plague victims. Saint Nicaise helped to protect against smallpox. Kings were views as people who were divinely appointed, and many thought that had the ability to cure skin diseases, scrofula, and other maladies by using the "royal touch."

In early Greece, China, India, and Egypt, this type of thinking was widespread, and rituals and incantation were done to ward off evil. Pandemics, bad weather, crop failures, other natural disasters were thought to be caused by either one person or a group of people who had displeased the gods. These people had to perform some sort of atonement. These beliefs are still prevalent in some communities.

In today's times, these ceremonies and prayers could be soothing and could help with the healing process but might not alleviate the condition or illness. Most of the time, a diagnosis from a physician was needed for problems that won't go away and were serious. Without knowing the cause for the condition because of prayer only, a wrong diagnosis, or not getting a diagnosis, the illness could get worse or be prolonged. This isn't trying to debunk using positive thoughts, prayers, or intentions, but relying only on these could do a huge disservice to the patient.

During this time, licensed medicine completely disappeared. The doctors who were still around were usually connected with an abbey or monastery. Even for these people, their goal wasn't to find the cause of the illness or even to heal it, but to study the work of other people. The Catholic Church banned surgery done by monks during the middle of the 7th century since it could damage their souls. Because nearly all surgeons at the time were monks, this decree put an end to all surgeries in Europe. Critical thinking wasn't taught or understood during this time. Aristotle, Hippocrates, and others had made a lot of progress in terms of critical thinking, but all of that ended up getting lost to the Western Europeans. All the talks about life and illnesses were based on theology with little to no scholarly influence. This was a very dark time for Europe.

Arab Influences

Let's move on and see how Arabs were able to save and expand on the sciences and medicine of the Greeks. During the time that Western Europe was falling into a black hole, the East experienced a surge in intellectual life.

Let's start this story in the beautiful and ancient city of Jundi Shapur. During 490 AD, their benevolent king had given shelter to the excommunicated Nestorian Christian scholars that had come from Europe. Many of these people were physicians. These people were Nestorius' followers. He was a patriarch that was tough during the Roman Empire. All these people were excommunicated due to heresy.

Before they settled in Jundi Shapur, they lived with the erudite monks in Syria. This area was meant to be a Macedonian colony. Edessa was located along the north edge of the Syrian plateau. It was known for being in the center of the "Silk Road to China." There was a medical school in Edessa where Nestorians worked and taught.

Zeno, the emperor during 489 AD, said it was a place that was full of heretics. He had the hospital closed, and they went on to Nisibis. They relocated to Jundi Shapur, which was located north of the Black Sea. The people who lived here welcomed the new arrivals after the closing of Plato's school in 529. Some of the Nestorians moved into China and India.

Since the Nestorians were scholars, they started the huge task of translating Greek books into Syriac. Galen and Hippocrates were part of their translations. These adventures helped to explain the reasons some of the Greek work was translated into a Latin version from Syriac. This is why Albucasis, Avicenna, and Rhazes, the great Arabic physicians, revered the Greek teachers and added their knowledge to East Indian medicine.

Many people haven't ever heard of Jundi Shapur, but this was where a lot of knowledge was promoted and preserved. Once the city feel in 636 to the Arabs, and Persia finally became part of Islam, they didn't disturb the university. The people who conquered it adopted it and used it as part of their training center.

Jundi Shapur's rulers welcomed all the Hindu, Jewish, Persian, and Greek scholars. All these people converging created a huge center of medical knowledge within the Islamic world for several hundred years. All of these people of various creeds worked together in harmony. This hasn't happened anywhere else in the world.

These Arab physicians made sure that they understood the work of Galen, Hippocrates, and all of the other prominent Greek physicians, and they were exposed to knowledge of the Chinese and Indians. Intellectuals, astronomers, physicians, and scholars of all branches of knowledge were asked to write, study, and debate about their works in this setting.

Near the end of the 10th century, Baghdad, which had become the capital of the Islamic State, started to drain the talents of Jundi Shapur. This end came extremely fast. Now, nothing remains of that wonderful city except for some trenches in the ground.

It needs to be said that most of these people used plants and exchanged plants from various localities and countries. This helped to expand these materials to other countries. The Islamic Empire soon stretched all the way from North Africa, Central Asia, Italy, Spain, and the entire Middle East. This allowed them to exchange plants.

Baghdad

Knowing how important it was to translate the Greek works into the Arabic language to make it more accessible, Harun al-Rashid and son, al-Ma' mum, created a bureau in Baghdad. This was named the House of Wisdom. This brought a better era to Arabic medicine. We can still feel the effects of this today. This was thought of as the great period of compilation and translation. This boom in development, inquire, and experimentation about all types of sciences was different from what Western European countries were doing. This was the Golden Age for the Arabic people.

The best translator during this time was Hunayn ibn Ishaq al-'Ibadi. He was said to have received a payment of gold for the works he created. He, along with his team, had translated the works of Dioscorides, Hippocrates, Paul of Aegin, Oribasius, and Galen, among others, into Arabic by the end of the 800s. Their writings created the foundation for unique Arab medicine.

Arab medicine followed the theory of humors created by Galen and believed the body was created from the same elements that make up the world: water, fire, air, and earth. All of the elements could be mixed in different ways could be used to help with the different humors and temperaments. If a body's humors are balanced correctly, the person will be healthy. Any sickness was caused by an imbalance in humors and not from a supernatural force. These imbalances could easily be corrected by a doctor's healing art.

Arabic physicians started looking at medicine as science where the body's temperaments could be recognized, and their goal was to preserve the health of the human body. If a person's health was lost, they had a way to help recover it. They looked at themselves as practitioners of the maintenance and healing of the body.

Advances had been made in many other areas. Harun al-Rashid created the first hospital, well, hospitals in the way that we know them now. In about a couple of decades, there were 34 more hospitals built throughout the Arab world. This number increased every year. These were amazing hospitals.

These hospitals didn't resemble the hospitals in Europe. The sick viewed hospitals as a place where they received treatments and could be cured by the doctors there. The doctors viewed the hospital as a place that was devoted to promoting health, curing disease, and expanding and distributing medical knowledge. Medical libraries and schools were soon attached to the larger hospitals, and the top physicians would teach the incoming students. These students were expected to use what they had learned to help the people in the hospital. These hospitals treated everyone no matter what their economic status or religion was. They had readings of the Koran, music, and gardens, and instead of giving the patients a large bill for their services, they provided the poor with money when they left the hospital to ensure that they had a better life as they were healing.

Hospitals also tested the students and would give them diplomas. By the 11th century, the hospital staffed traveling clinics. This provided medical care to people who didn't live close enough or were too sick to get to the hospital. The hospitals were the center of Arab medicine and were the prototype that modern hospitals were based on.

Just like hospitals, herbal pharmacies were developed by the Arabs. Islam teaches: "God has provided a remedy for every illness," and all people are able to search for all of these remedies and use them wisely with compassion and skill.

Jabir ibn Hayyan wrote one of the first pharmacological texts. He is considered the father of Arabic pharmacy. This text was very extensive and gave plants geographical origin, physical properties, and ways to used the plant to cure diseases. Arab pharmacists introduced many new herbal drugs to hospitals in the known world. Some of these new herbal drugs were mercury, ambergris, aconite, cloves, nutmeg, tamarind, cassia, myrrh, musk, sandalwood, camphor, and senna.

These pharmacists also created juleps and syrups. The word julep comes from the Persian and Arabic languages that mean sweet water that is made from things like orange blossom and rose water. They knew all the anesthetic effects of the Indian herbs that could be inhaled or added to liquids.

During this time, the pharmacist was a profession that was only done by people who have been trained extremely well. They had to pass several exams, be licensed, and had to be monitored by their state. During the start of the 9th century, Baghdad saw its first herbal apothecary shop. Pharmaceuticals were created and distributed through commercial means, and then given by pharmacists and physicians in various types like inhalants, suppositories, tinctures, confections, elixirs, pills, and ointments. Herbal medicines were beginning to reach a new level of usage and were being appreciated during this time in history.

Quick Review

In the beginning, the Arabs studied, compiled, and translated the ancient texts from Greek to Syriac, and to Arabic. They created learning centers where people from Western Europe, China, North Africa, India, and Persia would come together to exchange ideas about science and medicine.

By 800 AD, the boom of medical information had been infused with the original thoughts from Arabic medicine. This fusion could really be seen when Al-Razi started focusing on medicine. Some of his most well-known books are an encyclopedia of 25 books called *The Comprehensive Work* that would be translated into Latin. His entire life was spent finding information for his book. The book was supposed to be a summary of medical knowledge. He added his own observations and experience. He told physicians to pay more attention to what their patients and medical history could tell them instead of them just consulting the past authorities. His clinical skills were matched by him being able to understand human nature, especially as seen in a patient's attitude.

He said patients and doctors have to establish mutual trust. He thought that getting positive comments from a doctor could encourage patents, make them feel better, and speed up their recovery. But he did warn then that changing doctors could hurt a patient's health, time, and wealth. This principle about the patient-doctor relationship needs to be looked into by our current medical professionals. Herbalists need to remember the way their clients have built their trust up with time as we get to know their world.

Central Asia Avicenna

It wasn't long after Al-Razi's died that Abu 'Ali al-Husayn ibn 'Abd Allah ibn Sina, a Persian, was born in Bukhara. Later on, translators would Latinized his name to Avicenna. He soon became the Aristotle or da Vinci to the Arabs. His interests embraced statecraft, poetry, music, psychology, mathematics, science, astronomy, philosophy, and medicine. The physicians of his time called him "the prince of physicians."

His father was a tax collector, and he was so brilliant that he had memorized the Koran by the time he was ten. He then studied philosophy, physics, mathematics, and law. At the age of 16, he started to focus on medicine, which he believed was not that difficult. By the time he turned 18, he was famous as a physician, and he was asked to help heal the Samanid prince. His treatment was successful. Due to this, he was allowed access to the royal Saminid library. This was the best library of learning.

He created a huge body of texts that are known as The Arab Golden Age, where all the translations of every text from the Aristotelian, Mid- and Neo-Platonic, and Greco-Roman eras were talked about, revised, and developed by Arab intellectuals. During his life, he wrote about 450 texts on many subjects, and about 250 of these have survived. About 40 of his texts concentrate on herbs and medicine, and 150 concentrates on philosophy.

He is regarded as a pioneer in aromatherapy due to the invention of extracting essential oils and steam distillation that he used during his practice.

His biggest contribution ended up being the encyclopedia named *The Canon of Medicine,* which originated about 1025 in Persia.

This text is known for introducing the idea of syndromes when diagnosing certain diseases, clinical trials, introducing experimental medicines, introducing quarantines to limit spreading diseases, finding sexually transmitted and contagious diseases, studying physiology, and systemic experimentation. Avicenna was one of the first to think about microorganisms and described and classified many diseases. He also outlined their causes. Functions of various parts of the body, complex medicines, simple medicines, and hygiene were covered in his book, too. He was the one that figured out the tuberculosis was contagious. The Europeans tried to dispute this, but it was found to be true. He also discovered the complications and symptoms of diabetes.

Please remember that whenever you see the word medicine in this chapter that all these medicines were minerals, herbal plants, and parts of animals that were used to create medicine. Don't confuse this word with modern medicine that is mostly chemical compounds. His book included a definition for over 760 medicinal plants and all the various medicines you can get from that plant. During this time, he laid out the basics for clinical drug tests, and his principles are still being followed today. He was a wonderful herbalist.

His book became a standard reference for the Arab world. Up until the 1800s, his book was used as a teaching guide and reference. It was used much longer than most other medical books. The healing system he used was called the Unani Tibb that translates into "Medicine of the Greeks." This is something that still gets practice in the Middle East, Central Asia, and India.

The Arab scholars of the 12th and 13th centuries continued to elaborate and develop medicine farther than where the Greeks left off. The traveled far, drew from their own observations, and took expeditions just to find and identify plants. In their texts, we can find coral, elecampane, lesser celandine, euphorbia, horsetail, elder, umbellifera, Artemisia, chamomile, and teasel. It would be several centuries before this type of work would take place in Western Europe.

Reawakening of Europe

In the 1100s, Europe started to receive benefits from the Arabs work, and through this, tried to find its own heritage. Roman and Greek works had been preserved and then expanded upon by the Arabs and were finally making its way back to Europe. Hippocrates and Galen's work came back to the West by the North Africans and Middle Easterners. All the Arab medical texts had been translated into Latin, which was the language of the educated Europeans. Due to the Arabic intellects and scholars, Europe was finally recovering part of its past.

There were two big-time translators who worked to translates the texts from Arabic to Latin. One was Gerald of Cremona; he worked in Toledo. The other was Constantine the African. He was a very learned man and spoke three languages fluently. He was located in Salerno and worked in the cloister of Monte Cassino. It wasn't an accident that these men both lived within this transition zone. This is the area when the two cultures started to influence one another. It isn't a coincidence that Salerno was close to Sicily in Arab. Salerno became the first medical school during the Middle Ages.

Avicenna's text appeared in Europe at the end of the 1100s, and it had a dramatic impact. After being coped and recopied, it was soon set as the standard medical reference in Europe. It had 16 editions, and after several more years, it would pick up more than 20 editions. From the 1100s through the 1600s, it was considered the pharmacopeia of Europe. In 1537, The Canon became the required text for the University of Vienna. This is where herbalism in Western Europe found its roots.

Europeans thought of Al-Razi and Avicenna as some of the best authorities on the teachings that dealt with medicine, and the portraits of these men can still be found in the School of Medicine at the University of Paris.

The Arabs didn't just provide a line of medical knowledge within the Hellenic and Greek world. They also made sure the work was correct and expanded upon it before they passed it onto Europe, who had abandoned the old ways of observing and experimenting that had been created years before. Physicians of various religions and languages created a structure that can still be seen in the medical and herbal practices of today.

Herbalism continued on from this point, and, in a way, we are all herbalists and indebted to the people of these various times, regions, religions, and cultures from all over the world. Just saying that "herbal knowledge was stunted during the Middle Ages," or any other simple statements are being shortsighted. This has a lack of scope, diminishes its brevity, and is completely incorrect. We need to be more educated in our herbal history to see that in one part of the world where it might become stagnant, but there are other areas that are in their glory.

What exactly is "herbalism?" Haven't we been practicing herbalism for years without knowing it? How many herbs became known centuries ago in lands far away from us? Our herbal roots didn't die out with the Dark Ages, now where were all the herbalists tortured or killed. Our roots travel much deeper and into the richer critical thinking, curiosity, and intelligence of the Arabs, Persians, and Byzantine scholars. From all of these people, herbalism was created.

Where did we get elecampane, myrrh, nigella, ginger, thyme, rosemary, oregano, fennel, nutmeg, clove, and cinnamon come from? What could we herbalists do if we didn't have all of these medicinal plants that have come from all over the world?

Because humans are very forgetful, we might have created some limited philosophies about herbs, such as the things that we may or may not use and how we view ourselves in a historical context as herbalists, or how we envision ourselves as part of this multi-cultural heritage could end up clarifying our role in history. This can end up helping up to be more open to fresh ideas of what exactly being an herbalist means. Once we are able to embrace our history and not make up an imaginary history that has been based on rumors, we can finally see ourselves in a bigger scope for all human endeavors to know our place in the world with plants and each other.

CHAPTER 2

Knowing Your Environment

The first thing you need to have a good understanding of is your environment, especially your climate. This will help you to have a good understanding of what types of plants are native to your area. This way, you don't end up spending your entire day looking for a certain plant only to find out it doesn't grow where you live. We will focus mainly on North America.

North America can be divided into eight different climate types:

- Forest – has four different seasons with cold winters and warm summers.

- Coniferous forest – dry and cold with snowy winters and some warm summers.
- Mediterranean – warm temperatures with a lot of rain in the winter and fall.
- Grassland – cold winters with rain and hot summers.
- Tundra – winters are very cold, summers are warm with some rain.
- Alpine – snowy, cold, and windy. It stays winter from October to May, with temperatures staying below freezing. Summer lasts June to September, with the temperatures reaching around 60 degrees Fahrenheit.
- Rainforest – high temperatures with lots of rain all year.
- Desert – warm temperatures with very little rain.

Different plants grow naturally in these various climate types. Let's take a look at where these climates exist within North America.

Forest Land

Forest, which is sometimes referred to as deciduous forest, is located in the Eastern, United States. This stretches all the way up to the tip of Maine and down through Florida, except for the very tip of Florida, which is part of the coniferous forest. It also reaches across to the Eastern edge of Texas and up to Minnesota. All of New England and the South Eastern US is deciduous forest land. Parts of the Great Lakes area are also deciduous forest land.

The deciduous forest also includes part of Southern Canada. These lands are made up of broad-leafed tree forests. These trees shed the leaves each year, which is why this area is referred to as a deciduous forest. But this area also has some conifer trees, which include evergreens.

This area once occupied around 2,560,000 km2. It was dominated by hickories, chestnuts, and oaks that provided food and shelter for the wildlife in the area. During the 18th and 19th centuries, there were unprecedented changes that took place here. The forest was cleared for urban expansion, fuelwood, timber, and agriculture.

The deciduous forest if a type of "temperate deciduous forests." These types of forests occur across the world in areas that are mid-latitudes, the area that occurs between the polar and tropic regions, in Southwestern South America, Eastern Asia, and Western Europe, and Eastern US. They can easily be distinguished by cold and warm air masses that create four seasons each year. Trees will change colors and will lose their leaves in the fall as the temperature levels drip. Winters will often have low precipitation levels and colder temperatures, and plants and trees will become inactive. During the spring, precipitation and temperature levels will start to rise, which causes the plants to come out of their dormancy and new flowering and growth to start. During the summer, plants in this area will grow the most because they are fueled by the warmest temperatures and most precipitation during the year.

Coniferous Forest

The coniferous forest covers most of Canada, as well as Alaska and the Northern part of Washington state. Coniferous forests are mainly found throughout the temperate climate of the Northern Hemisphere. Around 85% of all coniferous forests are located in North American and Eurasia. It extends across the northern part of North America, through Russia and Scandinavia, and across Asia from Siberia to Mongolia, northern China, and northern Japan.

These forests are mainly made up of spruces, northern pines, Douglas firs, silver firs, larches, and hemlocks. These softwood forests create a resource of great importance and yield the bulk of pulpwood and lumber handled commercially.

Mediterranean

The Mediterranean climate is most commonly associated with the Mediterranean Basin, but there are other regions that have a Mediterranean climate. This includes the coastal area of the Western United States, mainly the outer edge of California, as well as the Western Cape of South Africa, central Chile, coastal areas of South Australia, and southern Western Australia.

This climate is characterized by dry, hot summers and wet, cool winters. These regions are normally located around 30 and 45 degrees latitude north and south of the equator. By and large, they are always located on the Western sides of the continents.

The annual temperature ranges in these areas are typically smaller than those in marine west coast climates because areas on the western sides of continents aren't positioned well to receive the coldest polar air, which is developed over land and not the ocean. They are drier than subtropical climates, with their precipitation totals normally range from 14 to 35 inches.

Grasslands

Grasslands are mainly found in the middle of large landmasses. Most of the mid-western part of the US is grasslands, along with the eastern part of Mexico. Grasslands are also found in the steppe that straddles Asia and Europe. Most of this clime is located between 40 and 60 degrees north or south of the equator.

This climate has a large temperature range between the hot summers and cold winters since this region is pretty far from the moderating effects of a sea breeze. Large temperature variations can occur in one place within a single day. Temperatures have the ability to change as much as 30 degrees from day to night. This difference is only beaten by the hot deserts. It has a rainfall total that ranges from 10 inches to 20 inches each year, which makes it a much wetter than the desert.

In North America, these regions are known as the Prairies. In Argentina, they are called the Pampas. In Asia and Europe, they refer to this region as Steppe. In South Africa, it is part of the Veld, and in New Zealand, it includes the Canterbury Plains.

This area has the best soil in the world, making it an important part of food production. This is why this land is normally covered in farmland. The one thing you won't see a lot of in this area are trees because it is too dry.

Tundra

The tundra is located in regions just below the ice caps in the Arctic and extends across North America, Asia, Siberia, and Europe. Around half of Canada and a lot of Alaska are part of the tundra. The tundra can also be found at the tops of the tallest mountains in the world. This area is characterized by extreme cold, but it can get warmer during the summer.

The winter in the tundra is cold, dark, and long, and temperatures stay below freezing six to ten months out of the year. The temperature gets so cold that there is pretty much a permanently frozen ground just below the surface that is referred to as the permafrost. This is the defining characteristic of the tundra. During the summer, the top layer of soil will thaw just a few inches down, which gives vegetation a chance to take root.

The amount of rain that tundra sees is less than the greatest deserts in the world, coming in at around five to ten inches. Even still, the tundra tends to be very wet because the low temperatures cause evaporation to be slow.

Alpine

The alpine climate is made up of mountainous areas. The Rocky Mountains, Alps, and the Andes are all alpine climates. The alpine can be found at an altitude of 10,000 feet, and where the snow line of the mountain begins. During the summer, the average temperature of this area ranges from 40 to 60 degrees Fahrenheit. During the winter, the temperatures typically stay below freezing.

As the altitude increases, temperatures typically fall. The temperature in this area is dynamic and can transition from warm to freezing in a single day. The winter is typically from October to May, and the summer is from June to September. This is a fairly dry climate, with the average rainfall being around 12 inches.

Rainforest

Rainforests are normally located across the world at the equator and are mostly found between the Tropic of Capricorn and Tropic of Cancer. This band is 3000 miles and is known as the tropics. You can find rainforests in Central and South America, Oceania, Africa, and Asia. Rainforests make up around seven percent of the surface of the Earth.

The largest rainforests are found in South America in the Amazon River Basin, in West Africa in the Congo River Basin, and throughout most of southeast Asia. You can also find smaller rainforests in Australia, Madagascar, Central America, India, and other tropical locations. Tropical rainforests have two seasons, the wet season and the dry season.

There are also temperate rainforests that you can find on the Pacific coast of the US and Canada, as well as Norway, Scotland, Ireland, Chile, Tasmania, and New Zealand.

Desert

Lastly, there are desert lands. One-fifth of the Earth is made up of desert land. A desert is characterized by a layer of soil that can be stony, gravelly, or sandy, depending on the type of dessert. They typically get about 20 inches of rain each year, and the things that live there have adapted to this dry climate.

Plants in the desert have learned how to conserve water. Cacti have enlarged stems so that they can store water, and their spines help protect them from thirsty animals. There are four types of deserts. They are hot and dry, cold deserts, coastal deserts, and semi-arid deserts. In hot and dry deserts, which are often called arid deserts, the temperatures tend to be warm and dry all year.

The most famous arid deserts are the Sahara Desert that makes up most of the African continent, and the Mojave Desert found in the Southwest part of the US. Semi-arid deserts tend to be a little cooler. The dry, long summers are typically followed by winters that get a little bit of rain. These deserts can be found in Asia, Europe, Greenland, and North America.

The Coastal desert is a bit more humid than other deserts. While they do get heavy fog that blows in from the coast, it is still rare for them to get any rainfall. The Atacama Desert of Chile is a popular coastal desert.

Cold deserts are dry, but their overall temperature is lower than most other deserts. The Antarctic is the most popular cold desert.

Now that we have a good understanding of the different climates that can be found in North America, let's take a look at what plants you can look for in each.

Edible Plants In Northeast US

The northeastern part of the United States is made up of nine states. They include Pennsylvania, New Hampshire, Connecticut, Rhode Island, Massachusetts, Vermont, New Jersey, New York, and Maine. If you refer back to the different climates that we just discussed, you'll notice that all of these states are a part of the deciduous forest climate.

You will notice that there is some overlap in plants in each of the regions of the US that we will discuss, as well as the climates. The one thing that you have to take into consideration is what area in the state you live in if you live in this area. While their climate is deciduous forest, cities, like New York City, have been so overtaken by people, you'll have to travel out of the city to really be able to forage for anything.

We know that the deciduous forest is characterized by all of its deciduous trees. These trees also provide homes for other plants here. Climbing vines, especially poison ivy, use the trunks as a support system. Mosses and lichens grew on the outer bark of the trees.

Below all of these trees are flowers and shrubs. The forest is broken into several layers of growth. The first is known as the shrub layer, where shrubs and bushes like rhododendron, holly, and azaleas grow. Shrubs tend to be deciduous and will lose their leaves during the colder months. Below this layer is the herb layer where wildflowers like

Dutchman's breeches, trillium, and bluebells grow. They normally grow in early spring before the trees have all of their leaves. Lastly, mosses, fungi, and lichens grew on the ground layer and take in all of the nutrients of the wet soil.

With that in mind, let's look at some edible plants that are easy to find in the northeast region of the United States. Most of what we will look at here are easy to spot, harvest, and consume. Also, most of them are beginner-friendly and hard to confuse for poisonous plants.

Cattail Root

Pretty much anybody will be able to recognize cattails. These plants grow plentifully in marshy areas, so they are most commonly found next to water sources. Its tall stature and distinctive tufted tops make them easy to see from a long way off.

You can pull the plants up by the roots and harvest the tubers. They can grow quite large, and some can even weight around a pound. These tubers can be dried and ground into flour, boiled, or roasted. They have a very mild flavor, so if it doesn't have a mild flavor, then I'd suggest you stop eating eat.

Dandelion

Everybody knows how to spot dandelions. Chance are, you have spent the better part of your life trying to kill them in your yard. They may even magically pop up through your sidewalk. If you don't know what they look like, go outside and look for the yellow flowers in your yard that will eventually turn into puffballs.

The flowers and leaves on the plant are the tastiest parts and can be cooked or eaten raw. Make sure you remove the green stem of the flower because it doesn't taste good. While dandelions can be bitter, especially when harvested in late spring and during the summer, many foragers are used to eating whatever they can find and think they are delicious.

Wild Garlic

Wild garlic is easier to spot during the early spring. It is one of the first plants that grow each year, so it isn't hidden behind other grasses. If you go only by how it looks, wild garlic can be confused with other species, even some that are poisonous. How to really know if it is wild garlic is to go by its smell. If you crush part of it and sniff, you are going to know you have picked the right plant. Both the leaves and bulbs can be eaten.

Watercress

That fancy stuff you buy to put in your salad can be found in the woods. Watercress is a peppery tasting green and is thought to be a delicacy. Chefs desire this green so much they pay people to hunt for it. You can find watercress in freshwater streams. You can eat the stems and leaves. Keep an eye out for floating plants that's leaves are comprised of small oval-shaped leaflets. When you harvest them, cut the leaves off and allow the roots to stay intact so that the plant can grow again.

Ramps

Ramps are coveted as well. These are wild onions, and they have a small but very tasty bulb and leaves. While they are hard to find, ramps grow in patches, so you will have a lot at your disposal when you find them. They are very sensitive to overharvesting, so only take what you need. You could even just harvest the leaves.

Nettles

The one thing that most people know about nettles is that they sting. This probably makes it seem strange that you would want to forage them. However, the sting goes away after they are cooked. Nettles are fairly easy to find, cook, and taste great. They do sting, so make sure you have some heavy-duty gloves when you harvest them.

Raspberries and Blackberries

A lot of people will tell you not to eat unfamiliar berries in the wild. You should listen to those people. Again, don't eat berries you are unfamiliar with. That said, raspberries and blackberries are familiar. You have likely already learned what they look like and how they taste from trips to the store. If you are confident in recognizing them, these tasty berries can be the highlight of your foraging expedition. Once you have spotted the fruit, you can enjoy the leaves on the blackberry plant.

Japanese Knotweed

You will have to forage for this in April. It grows into thick stalks that look a lot like bamboo and tastes like a cross between lemon and celery. Japanese knotweed is a rare opportunity in the foraging world. When you find it, even late in the season, it is going to regrow. This regrowth will give you another chance to harvest the plant in seven to ten days. But, Japanese knotweed is an invasive species that can damage local ecosystems. So eat all you want because you are helping the environment.

Goldenrod

This is fairly easy to spot because of its bright yellow color and the fact that it is several feet tall. It contains long, lanced leaves, and you can find it on the edges of most fields. It is most common during late summer and early autumn. The leaves and flowers are edible and can be eaten raw. You can also brew it in a tea. Make sure you turn the leaves over because the leaves are prone to toxic mold growth.

Milkweed

These plants grow in fields and in large quantities. When it is broken, it will ooze out a sticky substance that resembles milk. It has two distinctive features. It is the monarch butterflies' favorite meal, and it grows large, spiny, edible pods. These pods can be stuffed or boiled, and have an asparagus type flavor. Make sure that you pick the pods when immature, or you could get a mouthful of seeds and fluff.

Edible Plants in Southwest US

The southwest is mainly made up of Arizona, Nevada, New Mexico, and Utah. It also includes the Navajo Nation. This area is mainly desert and is home to some of the US's most amazing natural wonders, including Carlsbad Caverns, Arches National Park, and the Grand Canyon. This region is home to a mixture of different influences, including Anglo, Latin, Hispanic, and Native American traditions.

For those who have never lived in a desert climate, you might be quick to believe that you won't be able to find anything to forage there. If you ever find yourself stranded in the desert, you may just be able to survive if you can learn some of the most common edible wild plants. You'll be surprised that they are nutritious and relatively plentiful.

Tepary Beans

Tepary beans have something that is rare in foraging, a whole lot of protein. It is also one of the most drought-tolerant legumes, with edibles, flowers, beans, and leaves. You can find it growing up to three feet tall on the ground or climbing up something else. Keep an eye out for broad-leafed plants with long pods that look a lot like green beans. Don't harvest from the plant if it is immature since you will only want to eat the beans inside of the pods and not the pods themselves.

Pinon Nuts

You've hit the jackpot if your find pinon trees in the fall. Pine nuts are delicious and full of precious fats. To harvest them, lay a tarp out under a tree and shake the trunks to release the seeds from the cone. This may take a bit of work, but it will be worth it. You can harvest them in late summer, as well, but they will require you to dry or char the cones in order to get rid of the resin that seals the seeds in during this time of year. Pinon trees only produce a decent harvest every few years, so it's possible that you may spot a tree only to find that it doesn't have any goodies.

Yucca

This edible wild plant grows all throughout the southwest, but make sure you don't confuse it with yucca, which is an edible plant in Latin America. The yucca is a spiky, low growing shrub. It can not only be used as food, but it can be used as cordage and soap. You can eat its young stalks, seeds, fruits, and flowers.

Saguaro Fruits

You can easily spot saguaro cacti as they look like the cacti that all of the cartoons depict. The early summer is the best time to get saguaro fruit, but you can find fruit at any time of the year. Fruits are typically at the top of the cactus. You should only eat the interior. They have a refreshing taste. You will want a stick or something to knock the fruit off of the cactus.

Prickly Pears

This is another cactus with edible fruits. It isn't tall, so it won't be as difficult to harvest, but it is obnoxiously spiny, so you got to watch out for that. Not only that, but they are covered with glochids, which are tiny and hard-to-see spines that are nearly impossible to get off of your skin.

Make sure you never touch any are of the plant with your bare hands until the spines have been removed. You can do this by cutting out the nodes or burning them.

Purslane

Purslane is a succulent that does very well in sunny places, which is pretty much all of the Southwest. You can eat every part of the plant that grows above the ground. Keep an eye out for squat shrubs with round leaves and a reddish stem. It tastes like watercress and is better when tender and young.

One other plant that can be found in the southwest is one that we have already talked about, and that is nettle. Nettle can be found everywhere in the US except for Hawaii.

Edible Plants in Southeast US

The southeastern area of the United States consists of West Virginia, Virginia, Maryland, Tennessee, South Carolina, North Carolina, Mississippi, Kentucky, Georgia, Florida, and Alabama. Again, this area is made up of deciduous forests, except for the southern-most tip of Florida. That means all of the plants that we talked about in the Northeast section can also be found in the Southeast. But let's look at a few more.

Persimmon

This is also sometimes called the date plum. It is sweet when ripe, but tends to be sour otherwise. If it is green, it is not ripe, so you should leave it on the tree for a bit longer. The persimmon is orange-red to yellow-orange fruit. They tend to be on the small side, about a half of inch to four inches in diameter. Persimmons can be found in pinelands, dry woods, fields, meadows, and clearings.

Arrowhead

As the name suggests, this plant has leaves shaped like arrowheads. Attached to this is the tuber of the plant and looks like a potato. Since it looks like a potato, you can treat it like one as well. It is peeled, diced, and roasted. If you can't peel it, you can eat it with its skin on as well. No part of the plant is toxic. Arrowheads can be found in shallow water and canals. One of the best ways to find it is to wade in the water, and once you find the plant, just pull on it.

Wild Strawberry

We all know what strawberries look at. You can easily spot the flower before the strawberry is produced. The flower has white five petals and is about ¾ of an inch wide. The petals are attached to a yellow cone. This cone is what will start getting larger and thicker, before turning red when it is ready to be picked. They often grow in woodland borders, slopes, fields, and meadows.

Edible Plants in Northwest US

The northwestern part of the US is made up of Wyoming, Montana, Idaho, Washington, and Oregon. These states are a mixture of different climates, including coniferous forests, grassland, alpine, Mediterranean, and desert. That said, there are quite a few plants that you can harvest in this region. In fact, all of the plants we have talked about so far can be found in this area, even the plants from the desert. Let's take a look at some more plants that you can find in this area.

Asparagus

This plant will need to be harvested in the early spring when it is in its spear form. After a few days, it will continue to grow into what looks like a pine tree. The shoots taste best when cooked. Make sure you don't harvest from a plant that is younger than two years old so that the plant can get established. It is most commonly found growing in disturbed fields and near the road. Young plants can sometimes cause contact dermatitis.

Burdock

The entire burdock plant can be eaten, including the roots. You can eat the young leaves raw. The older leaves taste better when they have been boiled in water. The roots of the first year plant can be added to stir-fries or soups. You can also use the roots just like you would use a potato.

Catnip

While you may have only thought of this plant as something your cat goes crazy over, it is also a great plant for humans, but without the psychotic effects. It is part of the mint family and can be eaten raw or cooked. It is great as a seasoning or as a tea. It grows in disturbed dry areas.

Chickweed

This plant is common in most areas and can be spotted by a single line of fine hair that runs between the stem node. It tends to grow in lawns and disturbed spaces in montane and low regions. The plant is better when it has been cooked and tastes like spinach.

Chicory

This plant is better when you harvest them young, or it is growing in areas that are protected from direct sunlight. If the plant is older, cook the leaves in several changes of water. You can also eat the flower heads on young plants. The roots can also be eaten. Ground chicory roots are often used as a coffee substitute. Look for chicory in disturbed ground, from the foothills and the plains to montane areas.

Edible Plants in Midwest US

The Midwest region is made up of Wisconsin, South Dakota, Ohio, North Dakota, Nebraska, Missouri, Michigan, Kansas, Iowa, Indiana, and Illinois. The climate of this area is mainly grassland, but there are areas that fall into the deciduous forest climate.

This area is well known for its farming because of its fertile soil. It is common in these states to see fields of oat, wheat, or corn growing. That means there won't be a shortage of crops in this area of the United States when it comes to foraging.

Serviceberry

This is a perfectly balanced sweet fruit. These are best picked between June and August. There are several different types of this fruit, and they can be found on bushes, or, occasionally, on trees. None of them are poisonous, but some of them tend to be a bit dry and tasteless. When they are red, they resemble crabapples, and the bottoms of the fruit look like a dried-up flower. The leaves are smooth, serrated, oval, and alternate on the stem. The flowers will bloom in spring, then closer to summer, you will start to see the fruit. They taste kind of like a blueberry and a cherry.

Yarrow

This is a perennial herb that can be found in many different colors, from purple and pink to white and yellow. It grows to be two to three inches in height, with leaves that look very thin and hairy. They are shaped like a lance and cut into small segments. The leaves grow in a basal rosette and are alternate on the stem. It will bloom during the summer, starting in June throughout July. It likes sunlight, so it is most commonly found in open fields.

Wild Bergamot

This is a perennial herb that is part of the mint family. It has a two-lipped tubular flower on square stems. They often grow two to four feet tall and will bloom from July to September. They range in colors from pink, red, or lilac. Wild bergamot will often grow in woodland edges, clearings, and dry thickets. It prefers dry to slightly moist conditions.

Edible Plants in South Central US

The south-central part of the US is made up of Louisiana, Arkansas, Oklahoma, and Texas. This area is mainly grassland with some deciduous forest and desert. This area has a mixture of the plants that we have also discussed along with a few others.

Wood Sorrel

This plant has small, heart-shaped leaves and stems that have a sour taste. It can easily be added into salads or soups for an interesting flavor. You should make sure you don't eat this plant in large quantities.

Turks cap

The edible flowers on the mallow plant are sweet, kind of like honeysuckle, and the leaves taste best when they have been cooked because they aren't as tough. A dark red fruit will grow after the flower has fallen off and is known as the Mexican apple. It has a texture and taste similar to an apple. Turks cap has to be cultivated for gardens.

Autumn Sage

The orange and red variety of these plants all have edible, fragrant leaves and flowers that can be eaten cooked or raw. They are often steeped for tea or used to season food. It grows wild and is very commonly cultivated for landscaping.

Pink Evening Primrose

The stems and flowers of this pretty pink plant can be cooked like greens or tossed into a salad. They taste the best when they are harvest before the flower has a chance to bloom out.

This is not an exhaustive list of the plants you can find in each region of the US. As you have probably figured out, a lot of these plants will grow in just about any area, especially nettle, purslane, and dandelion. We will discuss many more plants in the coming chapters so that you can have a better understanding of what you can look for on your next foraging adventure.

CHAPTER 3

Compendium Of Edible Plants

We've already discussed quite a few different plants that can be found in different areas in the US. But to make sure you are prepared for your foraging trips, this chapter will be a list of edible plants that you can hunt for on your next outing.

Agave

Agave can be found in areas where the soil is sandy or loamy and well-drained. They do not like shade and tolerates drought. The flowers, sap, basal rosettes, and stalks can be eaten. The buds and flowers should be boiled or steamed before consumed. The flowers are great battered and fried. The leaves can be diced and baked or roasted. They have a rich caramel flavor.

Alligator Weed

Alligator weed can be found in California, as well as southern and southeastern states. They grow near water sources and form thick mats. They are invasive, so it is a rather abundant weed. It can be treated like spinach, but don't eat it raw. It has to be cook in order to kill off any aquatic parasites. It is full of minerals and a decent amount of protein.

Amaranth

Amaranth, also known as pigweed, can be found in most areas of the US and likes disturbed areas like edges of woods, yards, and fields. It tolerates most soil types, but it prefers rich soil. It grows near lambs quarters. Pick the smaller to medium-sized leaves because they contain more nutrients. Amaranth can be cooked like spinach, steamed, or sautéed. You should never eat his raw.

Apple

Apple trees can be found in any state that is within the deciduous forest climate. When it comes to foraging for apples, you can either pick them off of trees or pick of fallen apples. A tip, always cook any fallen apples you pick to make sure it is safe to consume. There are many ways to cook with apples. You can turn them into cider, apple butter, pies, and even your own apple cider vinegar.

Arrowhead

Arrowhead is a perennial aquatic plant. It grows fairly well in any area with a decent amount of water, such as streams, marshes, and ponds. The tubers of the plant can be eaten once boiled or roasted. They are typically roasted, and while the skin is edible, they are better when peeled.

Asparagus

Asparagus can be found in every state in the US, but it is still a rare plant to find. They have to be harvested in early spring. Depending on how quickly a state warms up, you can find them as early as February or as late as June. It does not like excessively wet soil but will grow close enough to water to get its benefits. It can grow to six feet in height and is ferny and resembles dill or fennel. You have to be quick at cutting the spears because they can send up early spears that fern out before you even find them. This asparagus is just like the kind you would buy in the store, so cook them however you would typically. They are great roasted and diced up and added to a frittata.

Bamboo

Bamboo is not native to the US, but has been introduced in many different areas and can become invasive. They can grow to 100 feet tall. Look for it in moist, warm areas, mainly within the southeastern US. Some are cold-hardy and can live in the north. Cut the bamboo close to the soil, or dig around the younger shoots, and cut them off just above the rhizome. Clean and then peel the outer sheaths. It is best when harvested in spring. Bamboo can be sliced into coin shapes, boiled, and cooked into stir-fries, soups, or meats.

Basswood

Basswood is full of fiber. The leaves can be used just like greens. The young shoots are also tasty. They can be eaten raw or cooked and can easily be used in place of lettuce in a salad. The flowers can be used to make tea, but they also produce a nectar that can create a great honey. Basswood is mainly found in deciduous forest areas.

Bee Balm

Also known as wild bergamot, it like sunny, dry areas as it can develop mildew easily in overly moist areas. It is a drought-resistant plant. The leaves and flowers can be eaten and are commonly used to help treat colds. It can be cooked or left raw. It is great in salads or as a tea.

Beech

The beech tree produces beech nuts, which was, at one point, a popular food source, but people have hardly heard of them now. They are found in the fall and are full of healthy calories. They have a spiky exterior husk that will pop open once they are ripe, which reveals two small nuts. The seeds will have a fibrous inner shell that can easily be removed once dried and cured. Beech trees can be found in the eastern US. The nuts can be used just like you would use any other nut.

Beautyberry

Beautyberries can be found all along the south and the southeastern US. They grow on shrubs that are about three to five feet tall. They are understory plants and are located in most wooded areas, especially when the soil is moist. Once they are fully ripe, the beautyberry can be eaten. They should be dark purple but not wrinkled. They have a slightly medicinal flavor. They are best when you use them to make a jelly. They can also be used to make wine. Limit how much you eat, though, they have been known to cause mild intestinal distress.

Birch

Different varieties of the birch tree can be found in the western and eastern United States. As an ethical forager, you should only take twigs, leaves, and catkins so that you don't kill the tree. They are minty and peppery in taste and rich in vitamin C. Birch is commonly used to make teas.

Bittercress

Bittercress grows in basal rosettes, and each stalk has around five to nine leaflet pairs. It is hardy and frost-tolerant and will stay green throughout most winters. Tiny white flowers show up during spring and will continue to bloom until fall. Bittercress should be used as quickly after harvest as possible because it wilts. It can be used in salads, soups, on sandwiches, and incorporated into hot dishes.

Black Walnut

The black walnut tree can be found in nearly every state in the eastern part of the United States. The walnuts are easily spotted by their large green shells. It's easier to grab the nuts when they fall to the ground, but make sure you get them before the squirrels do. You can use a knife to cut open the green hull, or you can place them under the wheel of your tire and run over them. Either way, be careful because the hull lets off a sap that can stain. Once out of the green hull, you can let them dry, or you can break open the shell now and remove the nuts. Use the nuts however you like to use walnuts.

Blackberry

Blackberries can be found all over the world. There are several different species of this plant, and they are all edible. There are a few species that don't have thorns, and you would be lucky if you came across these. When foraging for blackberries, be expected to carry home some scratches with you as well. It seems the largest berries are always right in the middle of the thorniest part of the plant. The leaves of the blackberry plant can help with digestive problems such as diarrhea. When the leaves have been dried, it makes a great tea. Ancient Greeks used it to treat gout and problems with the throat and mouth. Blackberries are full of vitamins and antioxidants but will mold if not kept in the refrigerator. Don't wash them until ready to use, as this will promote mold. These tasty berries begin ripening as early as June, but most of the time, somewhere near the end of July. If you pick unripe berries, they will not ripen once taken off the vines. Blackberry seeds are a great source of calcium, Omega 3 and 6, iron, phosphorus, and potassium.

Bladderwrack

Bladderwrack can be found on shorelines in central and northern California and along the northern coasts of North Carolina. It is a perennial seaweed that has a hard, flat root. The frond can range from a couple of inches in length to four feet. It is about an inch wide and has a flat rib that runs down its length. The "air sacks" will vary in size from the size of a pea to a marble. It is best to collect during low tide. It can be eaten cooked or raw. You can also dry it for later use. It has a very strong salty fish flavor. Bladderwrack contains fiber, protein, polyphenols, oleic acid, iodide, phosphorus, iron, manganese, selenium, magnesium, zinc, beta-carotene, B-vitamins, vitamin C, essential fatty acids, silicon, mannitol, cellulose, chlorophyll, zeaxanthin, lutein, potassium, sodium, bromine, mucilage, algin, and iodine.

Blueberry

Foraging for blueberries can be a gateway for foraging for other foods. These blue beauties are easily recognized. They are normally smaller than what you find in stores. They are scrumptious and seedless. These bushes won't prick and scratch you to death like raspberries and blackberries. They are full of manganese, fiber, vitamin C, and antioxidants. Wild blueberries are better than the cultivated ones. Wild blueberries are smaller and have a more intense flavor. There are two kinds of wild blueberries: low brush and high brush. Both of these can be found near low wet woodlands and lakes. They can be found anywhere in the world. Different countries call them different names.

Burdock

The roots of the burdock plant are very medicinal. Most people don't realize that you can eat burdock, too. The roots, stalks, and leaves are all edible and very tasty if you know how to cook it. Burdocks can be found at the edges of most walking paths where the seeds can grab onto animals and humans. Burdock is a biennial, so the roots can be harvested during its first fall or second spring. It is best to harvest the plant while they are young as a mature plant's taproot will be several feet long and about two inches in diameter. They can be quite difficult to dig up. Burdock can be found all over the world, and most people say it tastes just like eating dirt. It is normally peeled, thinly sliced, and added into stir-fries. Some people in the eastern part of the world just wash it, adds it to a pan of olive oil with some salt and pepper, and roasts it. They don't peel it. Burdock tincture is a great anti-inflammatory. Burdock vinegar is great for digestive issues. Just put some roots into a jar and cover with apple cider vinegar. Let it sit for a few months and strain. The "pickled" roots can be eaten.

Cattail

This is a very versatile plant that grows wild in most parts of the United States. This is a water-loving plant that grows on the edges of swamps, marshes, streams, and lakes. If you harvest this plant at the right time, the bottoms of the stems can be eaten raw or cooked. You need to make sure that the water isn't polluted. Never harvest cattails if there is a lot of human activities like riding horses, etc. There could be parasites or harmful bacteria in the water. These are best when harvested in early spring, but if you want to harvest the pollen, it is best to do this in May and June. Other than using this plant for food, the Native Americans use it to make woven baskets, sandals, roofs, and hats. The dried leaves can be used to make children's toys and dolls. The roots can be crushed and put on cuts, bruises, or burns the help with pain and to speed up healing. All parts of this plant can be eaten.

Cherry

Wild black cherry trees can be found throughout the eastern part of North America and into the lower parts of Arizona and New Mexico. They can be found south in Mexico and beyond. They have become naturalized in Europe. The black cherry tree can be used for landscaping, woodworking, and food. The inner bark can be turned into cough syrup. This fruit is important to the survival of many mammals and birds. Many songbirds eat black cherries during migration. Even though the fruit is edible, the seeds, bark, twigs, and leaves are poisonous to humans and livestock. They have a cyanogenic glycoside that will break down when digested that creates hydrocyanic acid or cyanide. Livestock gets poisoned when they eat any leaves that have wilted. Black cherries contain 17 antioxidants. It is a good source of melatonin and contains cadmium, zinc, selenium, copper, sodium, potassium, phosphorus, iron, magnesium, calcium, vitamin C, B vitamins, and vitamin A. It is still debatable if the seeds are edible or not.

Chestnut

The American chestnut is native to North America, but most of these plants were killed out by a fungus that was introduced during the late 1800s from the import of Chinese chestnut trees. About three billion chestnut trees were killed during this time. This tree still thrives in Appalachia, New Jersey, and Michigan. The nuts from both the American and Chinese chestnut are edible. The American chestnut will have their nuts encased in a spiny bur. These will open up and drip their nuts right before the first frost. They will contain two skins, a leathery outer hull that is brown and a papery like skin under this one. This was a very important food source for the early settlers, and most animals like turkeys and deer rely on chestnuts to get them through the winter.

Chickweed

Chickweed isn't a native plant to North America. The European settlers brought it over. Most gardeners hate it as it can quickly take over a garden, but it does contain more minerals and vitamins than kale or spinach. Chickweed likes rich, soft soil that is damp and cool. All parts of the chickweed are edible, the flower, buds, leaves, and stems. You need to be a bit selective when harvesting since only the top two inches of the stem can be eaten. Lower than that, and the stem is too fibrous and stringy. Just some scissors are all you need to harvest this plant. Chickweed is tender and can be eaten right from the plant or added to salads. It is a good source of potassium, magnesium, calcium, and vitamin C.

Chicory

Chicory is best known for its roots, but its flowers and leaves can be eaten, too. It can be found all over the world. It is normally harvested during the fall. Their roots can sometimes be hard to harvest since they like growing in packed soil. If you want to collect the roots, try to find areas where the soil is looser, but this might not be possible. Digging around the roots will increase your chances of getting a lot more. The root is edible and a great source of prebiotics and fiber, as well as insulin. It is normally roasted and used as a substitute for coffee. The leaves can be used just like dandelions in salads or cooked like spinach. The flowers can boost your immune system and could help you relieve some stress.

Chinkapin

Don't confuse this plant with an oak that has a similar name. They do have leaves that look alike, but the oak tree will give you acorns where the chinkapin will have a spiny burr that houses one to four nuts inside. The Eastern part of the United States has a chinkapin that is native on the East coast from New Jersey down and west to Texas. If you go foraging for this nut, please wear gloves as these spines can become embedded in your skin. Don't get fooled by a red berry on this bush as this is a gall that was created by the chinkapin flower gall wasp. If you are lucky enough and find some burrs, you can dry these out a bit to make the nuts easier to get to. Don't ever expect to get a large number of nuts if you do find a chinkapin bush. Timing is everything, and you might have to search for the burrs at the correct developmental stage.

Clover

This plant can be found all over the world. Clover has been used as a cover crop all across the world. You can even find it in the Arctic and Antarctica. Clover is part of the pea family. Every part of the plant from its roots to its blossoms can be eaten. The blossoms are pleasant tasting but not the other parts. When you are harvesting blossoms, don't pick any brown ones. You want fresh ones, whether they are red, pink, or white, even though the white ones are the tastiest. You can put them in teas or roast them. Young leaves can be eaten raw but no more than about one cup. More mature leaves need to be cooked. Clover has beta carotene, protein, vitamin C, some B vitamins, bioflavonoids, inositol, choline, and biotin. Just a quick warning here: some people might be allergic to clover and don't know it. If you do decide to try it, only consume a small amount until you know for sure that you aren't allergic to it. NEVER ferment any part of this plant. You want to consume this plant either totally dried or totally fresh: nothing in between. Last but certainly not least, clover that is grown in warm climates can contain a small amount of cyanide.

Common Violet

Violets can be found in North America, Australia, and Europe. Violets are a native species. They are essential for pollinators like bees. There are other colors of violets like yellow, lavender, periwinkle, white, magenta, and of course purple. They are a tasty wildflower but are only around during early spring. It has a unique aroma and flavor that has been enjoyed for hundreds of years. They were used in baked goods and candies until WWI. When roads became more prevalent, the areas where they grew were torn up. Its most famous use was in Crème de Violette, which is made by infusing violets into natural spirits. The leaves can be put into salads. It has a flavor similar to lettuce and sweet peas. The flowers have a unique flavor that is delicately floral and not as intense as roses. They can be put into salads, but they will get lost in all the other flavors. If you have huge amounts of flowers, you could make jam or jelly, but the flowers are best when infused into alcohol or made into syrups.

Cranberry

Wild cranberries can be found all across the northeast part of the United States and Canada. They are similar to wild blueberries, and they like acidic soils. Most can be found growing in dense patches along the edges of small ponds, swamps, bogs, and lakes that are cold. They will be ready for harvesting around October and September. They can be eaten straight off the vine, or you can bag them and freeze them to be used later. If you are lucky enough to find some, look close to the ground as the fruit likes to hide among the foliage. When you get your fruits home, give them a good washing. Get rid of any broken or bad one and throw out all debris and stems. Shake off the excess water and place them into freezer bags and freeze. You could also turn them into juice or compote.

Dandelion

Dandelions are quickly becoming known as a superfood. These beautiful yellow plants can be found all over the world. They are higher in vitamins than spinach and kale. They are full of antioxidants and vitamins. Just a half-cup of greens contains more calcium than eight ounces of milk. They are also a good source of vitamins K, A, and C. They are rich in potassium, too. They can help stabilize blood sugar and makes them a great choice for diabetics. Dandelions can lower cholesterol, manages high blood pressure, slows aging, and detoxifies the liver. Every part of this plant is edible from the bright yellow flowers to its root.

Dayflower

The dayflower was introduced to North America from Asia and can be found prevalent in Florida. There are some native North American dayflowers in a different genus. It can be confusing. Most can be found growing peacefully alongside spiderwort. The young tips and shoots are great fried, steamed, boiled, or as an herb. The flowers can be eaten right off the plant or added to salads. The roots can be eaten but get slimy when cooked.

Devil's Walkingstick

The Devil's walkingstick is native to eastern North America. The fruits and leaves are edible. This plant is a silly looking plant. It is a part of the ginseng family but doesn't have the qualities of ginseng. It is great for toothaches and rheumatism. Native Americans and southern herbalists use the berries and inner bark as a pain reliever for inflamed gums and sore, arthritic joints. Eating a few berries raw is fine, but if you want to eat more, you should cook them and turn them into jelly. They have a bitter flavor. You can also infuse them in liquor to help with rheumatism. Cherokees have used the roots as a salve to help will skin issues like boils.

Dock

Most species of the dock are edible, but the broadleaf and curly dock are the most common in the United States and Europe. The dock plant has a tart flavor similar to lemons. If eaten in large quantities, it could cause kidney stones like spinach. When the leaves are young and tender, they will have a more tart flavor. From early to the middle of spring, you can pick young leaves to eat either raw or cooked. You can sauté or boil the leaves to get the most out of their flavor. They are great in cream cheese, egg dishes, stews, soups, and stir-fries. Since dock has a short harvest time, harvest as much as you can and blanch, then freeze them to be used later.

Dollar Weed

Dollar Weed is a member of the carrot family, and you only eat the leaves. It has a taste similar to celery and carrots. You can use it to add flavor to stocks. You could also add raw leaves to salads. It grows prevalent in zones three to 11 in the United States and can be a rather invasive plant.

Duckweed

Duckweed can be found all over the world. It has a flavor that is close to sweet cabbage. Duckweed grows in poor water. It contains niacin, vitamin B6, vitamin A, vitamin C, five percent fat, 44 percent carbs, and 20 percent protein. This is an extremely tiny plant that looks like a meal floating on top of the water. You need to boil the duckweed, change the water, and then put them in smoothies, etc.

Elderberry

Elderberries can be found in Europe and North America. Elderberries can be helpful for flu and cold symptoms. Those beautiful white flowers that the pollinators love will soon turn into beautiful dark berries waiting to be made into cold remedies. The unripe berries, stems, and leaves are toxic to humans. Only use the ripest of berries. Stay away from the red elderberries as these are also toxic. Raw berries are a bit poisonous and could cause diarrhea, vomiting, and nausea.

Evening Primrose

Evening primrose is a biennial plant that is native to the United States and Canada. It has been naturalized in Europe, New Zealand, Australia, South America, eastern Asia, and Russia. It loves full sun and is drought tolerant. You can harvest the roots during spring means you will get succulent, sweet, fleshy roots. This plant can grow fairly large, and some roots will look a bit like parsnips. Once the roots have been washed, you can eat them raw. You can gather roots later on, but it won't be as fleshy. The leaves can also be used just like any leafy green. The flowers have an amazing taste and can be put into salads. The seed pods can be roasted and enjoyed. The stems when young can be used. This edible plant contains vitamin B3, potassium, calcium, beta carotene, carbohydrates, and protein.

Fiddlehead Fern

Fiddlehead ferns can be found in the eastern parts of Canada and New England. These plants only grow in wet areas. You will need to look along the edges of swamps, streams, and rivers. Fiddlehead ferns start emerging during the middle or late April or into early June. Check their locations weekly, so you don't miss your opportunity to harvest this plant. They need to be picked while the tops are still coiled tightly. The short stem is also safe to eat. Once you get them home, wash them well, and store in the refrigerator. Never eat these raw. They need to be cooked. They can be used in dishes just like any other green vegetable.

Field Garlic

Field garlic can be found all across the world. These can easily be spotted growing in the middle of fields, meadows, and lawns. If you know what chives look like, you won't have any problems finding these edible wonders. If you think you might have found a patch of field garlic, pinch off some of its leaves and give it s sniff. If it doesn't smell like garlic, don't eat it. Every part of this plant can be eaten. If the ground around the plant is a bit hard, you might need to use a hand trowel to dig around the base of the plant. You can use this plant just like you would green onions or chives.

Forsythia

Forsythia can be found all over the world. The pretty yellow flowers can be eaten right off the plant, but some say it is a bit bitter. It has several medicinal properties like a skin tonic or diuretic. It was used in China to treat strep throat, bronchitis, and colds because it clears the body from toxic heat like dermatitis, skin eruptions, chills, fever, and sore throats. The flowers can be dried or steamed, used as infusions or decoctions, or turned into teas. You can also toss the flowers into your spring salad for a bit of color.

Garlic Mustard

Garlic mustard is a common weed in North America and Europe that seems to find new territory in the United States. By April or May, you should be seeing this plant popping up everywhere. To harvest this plant, just pull the entire plant up. You will be doing the plants around it a favor as this plant can choke out native plants. Your main focus needs to be how many and the size of the leaves. If possible, find plants that are tall and have large leaves at the base. These give you more to work with. The larger leaves are not as bitter. Try to get only the leaves as the stems can be a bit fibrous and stringy. If you won't be using the leaves quickly, place them in water and store in the refrigerator. They will keep for a few days. You can eat the leaves raw or cook them like any other green.

Glasswort

Glasswort grows in brackish waters and salt marshes. It can be found in North America, Europe, and Africa. It is ready for harvesting by late summer. They taste similar to asparagus and can be used either cooked or raw. The easiest way to cook them is by either steaming or sautéing. Don't overcook them as it will lose its flavor. Glasswort contains bioflavonoids, iodine, calcium, iron, vitamin C, B vitamins, and vitamin A.

Greenbrier

Greenbrier is native to the United States but can be found in Ontario, too. When harvesting this plant, you need to get it while it is very tender. Just snap the tendrils off wherever they will break off cleanly. You can eat them just like they are, or you can chop them up and put them in salads, soups, or stews.

Ground Cherry

Ground cherries are related to tomatillos and tomatoes. They can be found in most parts of the world. The fruit can be either cooked or eaten raw. You could also turn them into preserves or pies. The fruit normally falls off the plant before it has ripened. It will take another two weeks until the husk has dried out, and the yellow fruit emerges. You can gather the fallen husks and ripen them at home. The fruit will store longer if left in the husk. If the fruit is green, don't eat it as it isn't ripe. If any fruit tastes bitter, you need to cook it first. If it still tastes bitter, throw it out.

Ground Ivy

Ground ivy looks a lot like dead nettle or henbit. It is a native of southern Asia or Europe but was brought to North America around the 1670s for medicinal uses. Ground ivy can now be found all across North America except for Nevada, Arizona, and New Mexico. Young plants can be added to soups and stews where the older leaves can be used for medicinal purposes and teas.

Groundnut

Groundnut is a member of the bean family but looks like a potato. They are native to North America east of the Great Plains. You can eat the shoots, flowers, and beans just like you eat regular string beans. The tubers are what is eaten the most. They look just like any bean that you might see in a garden, and they smell like a bean. The plant also grows beans that can be cooked and eaten just like regular beans. The tubers are what you are after. They can be harvested at any time that the ground isn't frozen. They do taste similar to potatoes but a bit sweeter but not as sweet as a sweet potato.

Hawkweed

Hawkweed is part of the sunflower family. You can find this plant across North America and Europe. The young shoots, leaves, and roots are what you want to harvest. The leaves can be eaten cooked or raw, and the roots can be roasted as used as a substitute for coffee. Hawkweed is full of antioxidants and minerals. Once the flowers have appeared, the leaves can be mashed to soothe insect stings and bites. The leaves can be turned into a tincture to be used as an appetite stimulant, fever reducer, or cough suppressant.

Hawthorn

Hawthorn can be found across most of the world. There are over 1000 species of hawthorn in the United States alone. Hawthorn is full of micronutrients, minerals, nutrients, and other natural compounds. It is the oldest known medicinal herb found in records dating back to the first century. Its main use was to treat heart problems but can be used as a tonic, an anti-inflammatory, immune-booster, or for digestive problems. They taste a bit like apples and make great pie fillings, jellies, and jams. The leaves of this plant are also edible and can be harvested in middle to late spring. The berries will be ripe during early or late autumn. When they are ripe, you can strip them from their branches, just be careful of the thorns.

Hazelnut

Hazelnuts are full of fats and protein, as well as tons of flavors. The American hazel grows over almost all eastern North America. The beaked hazel grows from the lower half of Canada down to the northern part of the United States. You need to harvest the clusters while they are still green if you wait, most of the nuts will be on the ground. Hazelnuts can be used like any other nut.

Hickory

Most of the hickory nuts found in the United States will be edible. This most popular one is the pecan that is limited to the south. In New England, the most common is the pignut and shagbark. When you have harvested your hickory nuts, place them in the sun for a couple of weeks before trying to break into them. The meat will shrink away from the wall of the shell, making it easier to remove. You can use hickory nuts just like you would any other nut.

Honeysuckle

There are more than 180 species of honeysuckle. These can be easily found growing along roadsides and hedges all across the world. The flowers of honeysuckle can be harvested and added to ciders and liquors to make a tincture. Honeysuckle has delicate floral notes. It pairs well with rose, elderflower, strawberries, peaches, sage, mint, yuzu, and citrus. Try using honeysuckle syrup in recipes rather than honey in a "Bee's Knees cocktail" with rum, brandy, whiskey, or tequila.

Hornbeam

Hornbeam is native to the eastern part of the United States. It makes great firewood, but be careful not to overload your stove as it can overheat quickly. The wood from the hornbeam can be used to make tool handles and sleigh runners. The bark and wood are medicinal. Infusions or teas that are made from the bark can be used topically for pains, including baths, to help relieve arthritis or muscle pains. You could use it as a mouthwash to help toothaches.

Horsemint

Horsemint is a plant that you have probably never noticed until you have learned to recognize it. It grows from eastern Canada south to Florida and then west to Michigan, California, New Mexico, and into Mexico. It makes a nice tea but can be brewed as a stronger herbal medicine. If taken in large amounts, it could be fatal. Whether you use it as a weak tea, strong brew for flu symptoms, or a poultice for arthritis, it is a pretty plant to have in your garden.

Horsetail

Horsetail is a perennial that grows in the Middle East, Asia, Europe, and North America. It is also known as the scouring rush or puzzle plant. Horsetail can be used to help strengthen tissues like bones, nails, hair, and skin, mucus membranes, arteries, ligaments, cartilage, and teeth. Horsetail can reduce inflammation and help strengthens lung tissue. It can improve bladder and kidney health by helping the body become resistant to UTIs.

Indian Cucumber

Indian cucumber is a native plant to North America. The roots or tubers and the leaves are edible. It does taste a bit like cucumber. It isn't very common, so please don't take too much as you can eradicate the entire species. They taste great in salads because of their fresh flavors. If you would like to eat Indian cucumbers, dig some up and replant them in your garden. The roots have anti-convulsion and diuretic properties. They can be brewed to make tea to stop seizures in children. The crushed berries can be made into an infusion.

Japanese Knotweed

Japanese knotweed can be found anywhere in the world. If you do find a patch of this plant, get as much as you want. You won't kill this out. Try to harvest the plants during the middle of spring when they can be broken off easily. As they mature, they will be stringy, and you might have to peel them. The roots aren't edible, so don't bother with them. If there are any pieces of the knotweed that you don't use, make sure you boil or burn them as it can root from the tiniest of pieces. Knotweed can be eaten as a snack, in salads, or raw. You can pickle or cook them like asparagus.

Jerusalem Artichoke

Jerusalem artichoke is native to the central part of the United States. It is a wild sunflower and can grow up to 12 feet tall. The tubers have been used for food by the Native Americans long before we came from England. The carbs in this plant come from insulin rather than starch. Harvesting needs to be done after it has flowered and before it frosts. It would be best to leave them along for several years so the insulin can convert to fructose. Tubers will be easier to digest and sweeter. Eating them too early can cause a lot of gas.

Mark the plants while they are flowering and then use a shovel to dig up the roots after the stalks have died back.

Jewelweed

Jewelweed is a native plant of North America. It can be used as an herb or as an antidote for poison ivy, oak, and sumac. The light green, young stems can be sautéed with onion and garlic and added to dishes like stews and soups. You could also add it to red beans and rice. They taste a lot like collards but are tenderer. Jewelweed can be used as an antihistamine and anti-inflammatory. Mix ground up jewelweed with some petroleum jelly and put in on the skin before your trek through the woods.

Kousa Dogwood

This plant is native to Asia but has been brought to the United States for ornamental gardening. The kousa dogwood has a taste between a mango and an apricot. There aren't many recipes for this out there, but I turned some into preserves and jams. They are a bit bitter when cooked, but I figured this was because of the skins. I rip them open and push out the gooey center. Push the goo through a sieve to get rid of the seeds to keep bitterness at bay.

Kudzu

Kudzu is a very versatile plant that we just don't use enough. Kudzu flowers smell a lot like the grape-flavored gum that children love. You can smell it from hundreds of feet away. Kudzu was brought into the US during 1876 as a part of the country's centennial celebration. Japan built a garden using Kudzu in Philadelphia. You can eat kudzu in several different ways. Young leaves can be eaten as is or juiced. You can dry them and put them in teas. Shoots can be cooked and eaten like asparagus. The blossoms can be turned into jellies or pickles. The root is an edible starch. Old leaves can be fried and eaten like potato chips. When cooking with kudzu, just let your imagination guide you.

Lambs Quarters

This is also known as wild spinach. It can be found everywhere in North America. Wild spinach goes a long way in describing its texture and taste. It is best to harvest the younger leaves as the older ones get bitter. The flower buds and leaf tips are a good choice for foods, too. These can be used as a substitute for asparagus or broccoli. You can use them in smoothies, omelets, stir-fries, and salads.

Locust

This tree can be found throughout the eastern seaboard and the Midwest. The blooms of the black locust are just available for a couple of weeks in late spring. The blooms look a lot like pea flowers, but they hang in clusters like grapes. Everyone will be a creamy white color. The seed pods are poisonous. The leaves and bark are also toxic, so make sure you get rid of any when you harvest your flowers. The whole flower is edible. When you have finished your harvest, leave your bag open so the spiders you have captured can escape. They taste a lot like sweet peas. And the base is a bit crunchy like celery.

Lotus

Some people consider the American lotus to be more American than apple pie. American lotus has been the main food source for Native Americans and can be found south and east of the Rockies and in parts of California. The young seeds, flowers, shoots, and roots are edible; it was the roots that the Native Americans sought after. This plant gives you phosphorus, calcium, potassium, sodium, and some minerals. The seeds are low in fiber but are a great source of oil. Seeds that are about half ripe can be eaten cooked or raw and taste very similar to chestnuts.

Mahonia

This plant is native to the western part of the United States. Its berries can be used in confections, beverages, jams, jellies, and pies. They can be fermented to make wine. The flowers can be used to make a drink similar to lemonade or eaten as they are. The young leaves can be simmered and eaten as a snack.

Mallow

It is most common in the Bay Area of California. The young leaves can be eaten in salads even though they have a texture that is interesting and isn't very flavorful. You can use mallow leaves as an herb in cooking. You can dry the leaves and then grind them into a powder and then add them to smoothies, soups, or gumbo type of dishes. This powder can thicken the dish. The immature seedpods or "cheese wheels" are great as a snack or similar to okra if sautéed.

Maple

These majestic trees can be found throughout North America. Sugar maples are famous for their syrup, but most people don't know that other maples can be tapped for syrup, too. Native Americans would drink fresh sap as a refreshing drink. The inner bark of all maples can be either cooked or eaten raw. The young leaves and seeds are also edible.

May Apple

Mayapples can be found in the eastern half of the United States between Florida and Quebec. The fruit is the only part of the plant that is edible, but don't let the seeds go down with the fruit. It has a taste between guava and pineapple.

Milkweed

Milkweed can be found in the eastern part of the United States and the southern part of Canada. The young shoots, pods, and leaves can be eaten once they have been boiled. The big question is, how many times do you need to change the water, and does the water need to be boiling when you put the plant in? Some so-called experts say you shouldn't eat this plant at all while others say it's fine, so who do you believe? You experiment for yourself but stay safe. If after you have cooked the milkweed, it still has a bitter taste, don't eat it. Just give it a taste and wait about 30 seconds, your body will let you know. Native American tribes ate the immature pods, buds, and young sprouts. Flowers were dried to use during winter.

Miner's Lettuce

Miner's lettuce can be found all over California. It was eaten a lot by the miners during the gold rush. They consumed it to prevent scurvy. They learned this trick from the Native tribes in the area. Miner's lettuce is a great source of vitamin C, vitamin A, and iron. It has a delicate flavor and a crisp texture. You can eat it just like any other lettuce. You can harvest and eat it at any time, but it is best to get before it flowers.

Mountain Mint

In spite of its name, it isn't a true mint but is closer to the members of bee balm. There are about 20 species, and all are native to the Northeastern parts of North America. The thin-leaved species are the only one edible. The wide leaved species have high quantities of pulegone, which is toxic to the liver and repels insects. It is great to keep mosquitoes away but not great for the tummy. The flowers and leaves can be used in teas or potpourri. They also work great in bathwater.

Mulberry

Mulberry trees can be found in North America in zones five through nine. If you are ready for purple fingers, find a mulberry tree, and pick all the fruit your heart desires. You could place a cloth under the branches and shake the branch. The berries will fall off, and you have your harvest. Give them a couple of baths under cool water to get rid of any bugs or leaves. They don't keep well, so eat them quickly. They can be made into pies, jams, puddings, ice cream, and cocktails.

Nasturtium

You can enjoy the leaves and flowers of this pretty flower. Most people enjoy them raw and added in salads. They have a peppery taste. They are native to South and Central America, but they can be easily grown just about anywhere.

Nettles

The big thing to remember with nettles is that they sting, so wear gloves. Nettle grows pretty much everywhere, except Hawaii. They like stream banks and disturbed areas. They are better before they flower. You need to blanch or steam them to get rid of the sting, and then you can use them like any other green.

Oak

The oak tree makes acorns, and acorns are edible. These trees can be found in eastern North America. All acorns are edible. Place the acorns in a water bath. Get rid of any that float. Once soaked, dry them. Crack them open using a hammer and woodblock. Late September through October is the best time for acorns. Once shelled, you'll want to soak the acorn in several water baths to get rid of the tannins. You can dry it out again and make flour or nut butter with your acorn.

Parsnip

The wild parsnip can easily be confused with the wild hemlock, which is poisonous. You need to make sure it has a flower because that's when it can be more easily identified. You can cook a very small amount of the plant to test it, and if it tastes bad, don't eat it. If it tastes bad, then there could be toxins. Cook them just like you would carrots are parsnips.

Partridge Berry

The leaves and berries are the edible parts of the partridge berry. Leaves are often made in a tea. The berries can be used in any type of culinary dish, although they do tend to be bland. They can be found in rocky and sandy areas. They are also found around red maple swamps and bogs. It is most common in eastern North America.

Passion Vine

Also known as a maypop, passion vines can be found in the southeastern region of the US. They are fairly common. You can use the leaves, juice, ripe fruit, and flowers. They are often used to make tea, preserves, drinks, and the fruit can be eaten raw.

Pawpaw

Pawpaw trees are common in eastern North America, especially in the Appalachian region. Finding fruit in the tree is a little more luck of the draw. They are ready to be picked from August through October. For some, raw pawpaw's don't sit well on their stomach. They are great turned into ice cream or pudding.

Pear

Wild pears aren't as easy to find as apple trees are, but they're out there. They look just like the pears you are used to and can be found in the same areas as apple trees. You can eat them like it is, or you can cook with them just like you would any pear.

Pecan

Pecans, like most nuts, have an outer hull that has to be removed and then a shell you have to get rid of before getting to the nut. Pecan trees are common all over Texas and in other similar climates. The hull will naturally be shed later in the season, but make sure you pick the nut off the ground before the wildlife has a chance to grab it. You can use the pecans just like you would use the ones you buy from the store.

Peppergrass

This is a native species in the mustard family. Its flavor tends to sneak up on you. The seedpod is the best part of the plant. They have an arugula-like flavor. You can dry out the peppergrass for winter use. You can use it just like any other seasoning. It is native to most of North America.

Persimmon

The wild persimmon is one of the last fruits ready to be picked in late fall and early winter. Persimmon trees grow in full or partial sun, and they like infertile soils. Fruit should be harvested when they start to wrinkle. You can enjoy them raw. You can also use it in desserts and preserves just like you would with other fruits.

Pickerel Weed

This plant is found in eastern North America as well in Argentina. It is also in Oregon. The seeds can be cooked or eaten raw. It can also be boiled and eaten like rice. You can also dry it and turn it into a flower.

Pine

Pine nuts come from pine, or pinon, trees. They are expensive to buy because they are hard to gather. Pine needles can also be eaten. They can make a great tea, or mixed into a recipe for a spicy kick. Pine trees can be found in most areas o the US, specifically in coniferous forests.

Pipsissewa

This oddly named plant can be found in almost every state except for the central southern and Midwest states, as well as Florida and South Carolina. It prefers the dry woods. Only the leaves of the plant are used, but they are tough and unpalatable. They are best used to make a tea.

Plantain

The young leaves can be eaten raw in a salad, or you can cook it. They are full of vitamin B1 and riboflavin. It prefers sunny areas and grows in most areas in the US.

Pokeweed

First, be careful with pokeweed because it can be toxic if misused. Young shoots can be boiled in two changes of water and will taste like asparagus. Poke berries can be cooked, and the liquid can be used to color canned veggies and fruits. Do not eat the berries; they are poisonous raw. It commonly found in central and northern North America. It found in rich soils.

Prickly Pear

Prickly pear is a cactus, so it is only found in desert climates. You can find them in the store labeled as nopales. If foraging for them, make sure you have gloves and carefully remove the spines and glochids, which are tiny hairs that are hard to get out of the skin. You can roast them, or eat them raw. Just make sure you get rid of the glochids.

Purple Dead Nettle

These are only available during early spring, so make sure you grab some while you can. It is a mint and is commonly confused for ground ivy and henbit, but of which are edible. It is easy to spot with its purple tops and grows just about anywhere, especially in your yard. It is commonly dried and used to make tea.

Purslane

Purslane grows everywhere fairly easily. It is considered an invasive weed in most of North America, so it is a sustainable plant to forage. There is a deadly lookalike, the potentially deadly spurges. The main thing to remember is that purslane will not have a milky sap. You can use purslane just like any other green.

Queen Anne's Lace

Also known as the wild carrot, is biannual. The first year it sends up the flower stalk and goes to seed in the second. You can harvest the roots during the spring or fall of the first year. The wild carrot can be used just like the garden carrot.

Ramps

These are some of the earliest wild edibles you can find. They will occur in higher elevations in eastern North America from Canada to Georgia. You can easily spot them by their broad leaves. Ramps can be found under the dense deciduous forest canopy. They can be used just like any other onion, but keep in mind, they are stronger.

Raspberry

Raspberries will start to ripen during the first part of the summer. They can be found all over the US. You can use the leaves and berries. The raspberry leaves are particularly helpful to women and can be made into a tea.

Redbud

The Eastern redbud tree is native to Eastern North America. In the spring, the flowers become a bright reddish-purple that can easily be seen. You can harvest the flowers and use them to make syrup, jelly, and cakes.

Rivercane

This is an uncommon plant, so forage wisely. You can use the seeds and young shoots and should be cooked or steamed. They can be found at river banks and are found throughout most of the south and eastern parts of the US.

Rose Hips

Rose hips start forming in late summer and through fall. Rose grows wild in most places, so you should be able to find the hips. Hips only form where the flower was, so if you have your own roses, don't cut them. Rose hips can be used as a fruit and dried to make tea.

Sassafras

This is a deciduous tree found in eastern North America. It has been used for many years to cook with, but be careful because it does contain safrole, which is toxic. The bark can be made into a tea. The root is most commonly used and was used to make the first root beer.

Serviceberry

These are native to North America. They taste like a cross between a grape and blueberry. They are easy to spot because there aren't any lookalikes. The smooth gray bark and have a showy, star-shaped white flower. They can be used as a substitute for blueberries.

Shepherd's Purse

This green shows up in early spring. Before the flower stalks appear, the leaves are great in salads or cooked like greens. They are in the mustard family. They often grow in grain fields, lawns, and gardens. The leaves can be a cabbage and cress substitute.

Smartweed

True smartweed will be very peppery. If it isn't, then it isn't smartweed. It is common throughout North America. It is best to soak the leaves in several water changes before cooking it. They can be added to salads or used just like you would other greens.

Sorrel

Sorrel is normally found in your lawn in most areas in North America. All you need to do is pull some of the upper parts of the plant off, or strip away some of the uppermost leaves. You can cook up sorrel just any other green.

Spicebush

The leaves, twigs, and berries are edible. The spicebush is commonly found throughout most of eastern North America. It is an understory shrub of moist forests and likes medium and light shade and rich soil. The twigs and leaves are often made into a tea. Only the female plant will produce bright red berries. The berries aren't used much because they don't grow in abundance, and they tend to rancid due to their fat content.

Spring Beauty

Spring beauty is part of the same family as purslane and can be used in a similar way. It is commonly found in the eastern 2/3's of North America. The plant prefers a dappling of the sun in the spring, and moist to slightly dry conditions. It can take a while to collect spring beauties due to their small size.

Sumac

The young shoots and roots can be peeled and then eaten raw. You can also eat the fruit raw, cooked, or made into a lemonade-like drink. It is a deciduous shrub native to North America and can be found in all mainland states and in southern Canada. It can be found in thickets, roadsides, and open fields. It tends to be invasive.

Thimbleberry

The thimbleberry belongs to the same family as blackberries and raspberries. While botanists would not call them berries, and refer to them as drupelets, we will simply call them berries. You normally can't find a whole bunch of them, and the bushes are normally small, but you can find enough to make some jam. They can be found in the same areas as raspberries and blackberries.

Thistle

Most places have a thistle plant, but the most common is bull thistle. They like areas with plenty of sun and little traffic and can grow to five feet tall. You can dig up the roots and cook with them. If you don't like the taste of burdock root, you may prefer thistle root. All of the thorns have to be removed from the leaves and the plant before you can cook with them. Most people find that the leaves are worth the work of removing the thorns. Make sure you think about using eye protection, as the thorns can cause a lot of damage. Remove all of the leaves from the stalk and then rack the thorns off of the stalk. These are good added to a soup. The flower can also be used and as an artichoke-like heart in the center.

Watercress

This wild plant is full of vitamins and minerals. It has a mildly hot must flavor, and is great on sandwiches or in salads. You can take the seeds and grind them into a powder to make mustard. It is often found near springs and brooks.

Wild Garlic

Wild garlic can easily be found by its distinctive scent, so you can't confuse it with anything else. It is best to harvest just the greens and leave the bulbs so that they can come back the next year. You can use the greens to make a tasty pesto. You can typically find some type of wild garlic in every part of North America.

Wild Grape

The wild grape is a vine, so it does not have a solid, upright trunk. It is a climbing vine and can completely envelop trees and bushes. It can grow in many different areas and all over the world. The grapes start as tiny white flowers and develop into green grapes. You can enjoy the grapes as soon as they form, but they taste better after the first frost. They are great in salad, or you can make your own jelly with them.

Wild Lettuce

This is a common plant in North America and is often viewed as a noxious weed in cracks in sidewalks, fields, and in yards. It is normally tall and had dandelion-like leaves. Some types will have yellow to reddish-yellow flowers. Since it is typically prickly, it is best if you cook it slightly first, or at least blanch it. Otherwise, you can use it similar to how you would use regular lettuce.

Wild Onion

Wild onions or ramps are some of the best wild foods during the springtime. Ramps have large wide leaves, and fairly easy to spot, especially in Eastern woodlands where they sometimes carpet the forest floor for acres. Some wild onions aren't as easy to spot. You can find some type of wild onion in any area of the US. They all send up grass-like shoots. If you see grass that looks like an onion, pinch a piece and sniff your fingers. If it smells like onion or garlic, then it is like a wild onion. There are plenty of poisonous plants that look like onions, but none of them will smell like one as well. They can be used just as you would use any type of onion.

Wineberry

Wineberry is one of the most abundant brambleberries. It is often placed on the invasive species list, and luckily they are also tasty. You can look for the wineberry around the same time as the blackberry season. They prefer full to partial shade and can be found in clearings, edges of fields, and in parks. They are orange-red and look similar to a raspberry. You will get sticky while picking them. You can enjoy them fresh, but they also make delicious baked goods and preserves. You can also make wine from them.

Yarrow

Yarrow is commonly used as a tea and is often taken before bedtime because it can help with insomnia. Dried, it can be used to flavor any dish that you would like and is similar in flavor to sage. It is commonly found in meadows, pastures, and old fields in eastern and central US and Canada.

Yaupon Holly

Yaupon holly leaves are normally dried and used for tea. You can find them all year, and they contain antioxidants and caffeine. The berries should be avoided because they can make you sick. Make sure you don't confuse it for the toxic Chinese privet. It is common in the southeastern US.

CHAPTER 4

Compendium Of Medicinal Plants

Many of the edible plants are also medicinal and can be used to help treat common ailments. They should not, however, replace modern medicine, especially for medical emergencies. When you are out foraging, keep an eye out for these medicinal plants to take home and enjoy.

Agrimony

This is a Chinese herb that is commonly used to stop bleeding. It is not as commonly used today but has its place in herbalism. It is safe in moderation for healthy people. It has neuroprotective properties, anti-inflammatory, and antioxidant. Agrimony contains tannin and volatile essential oil. It has an astringent action and is commonly used as a mouthwash ingredient. It can be applied externally to heal ulcers and sores. It grows in the US, Canada, and Europe. Its natural habitat is fields and woods. It has one to two-foot branched stems covered with silky, fine down and yellow flowers.

Aletris Farinosa

This is an uncommon wildflower with grass-like leaves. It is also known as ague root, true unicorn root, colic root, and star grass. It has commonly been used to help with female-specific health complaints. It can become toxic if too much is ingested. Since it is rare, it likes to be a protected plant in most places because cultivation is difficult.

Angelica

Angelica is commonly used in herbal medicine. It is a great tonic for children and women, as well as the elderly. It is believed to help strengthen the heart. Powdered angelica root is believed to cause disgust for liquor. It can help prevent the growth of bacteria. It can also be used for obstructed menses and shouldn't be taken in large amounts by women who are pregnant. An infusion can be used as a gargle for sore throats. It can be used as a wash for the face to prevent acne. The fresh angelica root is not edible and can be poisonous. Angelica contains glucose, fructose, iron, magnesium, potassium, riboflavin, sucrose, thiamine, zinc, and vitamin B13. It is a biennial native to Eastern North America. It can be found in thickets, moist cool woodlands, bottom-lands, and shady roadsides.

Black Cohosh

This plant is a giant member of the buttercup family and is native to North America. Chinese and Native American herbalists used this plant for many different ailments. Women will often use black cohos to help treat the symptoms of menopause, and it can help with cramps and induce labor. Be careful; in large doses, black cohosh can damage the liver.

Bloodroot

Bloodroot is commonly used in herbal medicine in small doses for throat infections and bronchial complaints. It is commonly used in different pharmaceuticals, mixed with other items to help treat heart problems, dental uses, and to help with migraines. A paste made from bloodroot can help to treat tumors, warts, and other skin diseases. You can even find bloodroot salve for this purpose. It is most commonly used externally, but when taken internally, you have to be careful because it has opium-like alkaloids, and an overdose is possible. It is native to North America and can be found in moist woodlands.

Blue Cohosh

This attractive woodland herb is become endangered because of over-harvesting. It rarely grows more than two and a half feet. In Tennessee, it will bloom in early April and is commonly found on wooded slopes. It has historically been used as a uterine tonic and to help with difficult labor. Its seeds can be used as a substitute for coffee. The berries are poisonous, and any part of the plant you want to use for medicinal purposes, do so under the advice of a qualified herbalist and medical practitioner. Pregnant women should not consume.

Butterfly Weed

This is an edible plant that is commonly used by herbalists. Also known as pleurisy root, it can be used as a vasodilator, tonic, expectorant, diuretic, diaphoretic, carminative, and antispasmodic. The root has been used to help treat rheumatism, dysentery, and diarrhea. It is a valuable herb for anybody how has lung problems. A poultice of the plant can be used to treat skin ulcers, wounds, bruises, and swellings. Too much butterfly weed can become an emetic. The seed pods are edible. Cook them when they are young and harvest them before the seed floss forms. The flowers are also edible when cooked. It can be found in Eastern North America. It is often found in dry open fields and grassy places.

California Poppy

The California poppy does not have any opium in it, nor does it have any addictive qualities. However, it can be used to treat similar problems that regular poppy can help. It has milder tranquilizing and pain-relieving problems. Instead of creating psychological problems that opium poppies can cause, it is mentally stabilizing. It is normally used as a tincture since the infusion is often bitter. The above-ground parts are normally harvested during the flowering period. Make sure you don't use California poppy before driving or any similar tasks until you are familiar with what it can do. It tolerates dry, hot conditions very well. It is common in California and is the state flower.

Chamomile

This is one of the most common tea ingredients and can easily be found in the grocery store. It has a mild sedative effect and is an effective treatment for insomnia and other nervous conditions. There is a small risk of allergy, but it is generally considered one of the safest herbs. It can also be sued to relieve gas and menstrual cramp. It can also be used as a mild laxative. It can also be used to help with allergies, the flu, and colds. It is also commonly mixed into lotions and soaps to help soothe irritated skin. It is effective for softening the skin, and relaxing tired, achy muscles.

Cleavers

A word to the wise, fresh cleavers plant can cause contact dermatitis for some. You should wear long sleeves and gloves when harvesting. It has been used to help cleanse the lymph and blood system. It is considered a diuretic, so make sure you stay hydrated while using this herb. It should be cooked down or processed in some ways before using it. Cleavers can be found worldwide, and nobody really knows where it originally came from.

Echinacea

Also known as purple coneflower, it has been used for many years in herbalism to help support the immune system. It is a popular herb taken during the cold and flu season. Echinacea extracts have been found to improve the cellular immune function in healthy people and in patients with AIDS. It doesn't fight off bacteria but makes the immune cells more efficient in fighting off the bad cells. It can be found in most states in the eastern US.

Ginkgo Biloba

The Chinese have been using this plant for well over 5000 years. It has been linked to alternative medicines for asthma, Alzheimer's, kidney disorders, heart disease, and to build energy. It is an adaptogen, which can help the body out during stressful situations.

It is a perennial deciduous tree native to China. Ginkgo Biloba is one of the oldest species of trees on earth and dates back more than 300 million years.

Ginseng

Ginseng has a long history of herbalism that dates back to 5000 years and appears on several continents. It has been extensively used in Native American medicine. It is another adaptogen and can help the body adapt to emotional and mental stress, cold, heat, fatigue, and even hunger. Ginseng is often one of the ingredients in energy drinks, but it is not actually safe to combine ginseng with caffeine as it will accelerate the caffeine's effect on your body and can end up causing diarrhea. It is a perennial herb in eastern North America. It likes rich soils and cool woods, but check your local laws for when you can harvest ginseng.

Goldenseal

Goldenseal is actually endangered in the wild, so you should try to cultivate it on your own and not harvest it. It can be used for short periods of time as an antibacterial, antiseptic, and antispasmodic. It is often made into a tea for upset stomachs and other digestive issues. It can also be made into a mouthwash for mouth ulcers, pyorrhea, or sore gums. It is native to eastern North America.

Joe Pye Weed

Historically, this plant has been used to treat fluid retention, gallstones, and rheumatism. The roots are the most potent. The flowers and roots are commonly used to make tea to relieve urinary and kidney problems. It can also be used to induce sweating and break a fever. It is come in eastern and southern parts of North America and prefers moist meadows and woods.

Lemon Balm

This is a medicinal and edible herb that can be added to salads or other dishes. The entire plant can be used, fresh or dried, to make warm relaxing teas and refreshing drinks. It contains volatile oil citral and citronella, which can help calm the nerves, relieve insomnia, menstrual cramps, and depression, and can relieve colic in babies. It is common throughout Europe and is mainly cultivated in the US. It can be found in sunny fields and is easily cultivated by cutting or seed.

Lousewort

Also known as wood betony, it is an edible and medicinal herb that was commonly used by Native Americans. It is prized for its aphrodisiac and medicinal qualities. You can apply a poultice of the herb to sore muscles, tumors, and varicose veins. A tea can be used to treat bronchitis, cough, tonsillitis, and a sore throat. It is native to eastern North America and can be found from Nova Scotia to Manitoba, and south to Northern Mexico and east to Florida. It likes moist thickets and woods.

Motherwort

This has become known as a woman's herb, which can be helpful in all stages of life. It can be used to treat heart palpitations, nervous pain, and menstrual cramps. It can also be helpful in lowering blood pressure and has hypotensive properties. It can be easily grown from seeds and reseeds itself profusely. Motherwort likes moist ground and blooms in midsummer.

Mugwort

Mugwort has been used for years in herbalism. It has antispasmodic, antibacterial, nervine, purgative, diaphoretic, tonic, diuretic, and digestive properties. A tea made of the flowers and leaves can help matters of the digestive system. It is native to Europe, Asia, and Africa, and has been naturalized in many areas of the world. It can be found growing around hedgebanks and waysides.

Mullein

In many countries throughout the world, mullein is a proven medicinal herb and has been back by scientific evidence. It can be used as a sedative, hypnotic, fungicide, estrogenic, cardio-depressant, bacteriostatic, antiviral, antioxidant, anticancer, anti-inflammatory, antihistaminic, and analgesic. It can be found all over Europe, in temperate areas of Asia, and in North America. It can be found on hedgebanks, and most often on chalk, sand, or gravel areas. It likes dry, uncultivated soil.

Soapwort

This herb has been used is the time of Dioscorides. It can be used as a tonic, purgative, expectorant, mild diuretic, diaphoretic, depurative, cholagogue, and antiscrophylatic. It can be applied to the skin to help with itchy skin. You can also obtain a soap by boiling the whole plant, especially the roots, in water. It is great for delicate fabrics that can be hurt by synthetic soaps. Do not take in excess as the plant can destroy your red blood cells.

It is a perennial in Europe and has been naturalized in the US. It can be found in moist ditches, meadows, and near old home sites.

Spearmint

This edible herb can be used cooked or raw. It has a very strong flavor and is commonly used in teas, which leave the body feeling clean. It can also be used to make mint jelly. The essential oils are commonly used to flavor candy, gum, drinks, and ice cream. It is great for using as an antiseptic, to ease stomachaches, and as a diuretic. It is found in Central Europe and has been naturalized in the US and Canada. It likes damp, sunny places.

CHAPTER 5

Compendium Of Poisonous Plants

The most important thing to be aware of when you are foraging is poisonous plants. Foraging should be something fun, and possibly getting sick or dying from foods you have foraged isn't fun. Let's go through some poisonous plants that you should avoid at all costs.

Angel's Trumpet

This is a distinctive woody bush with trumpet-shaped flowers that hand like bells. They are most fragrant at night. It is a common ornamental plant in the US, so you probably won't find it in the wild. While beautiful, they can kill you if you eat it.

Castor Bean

The castor bean contains ricin, which is the most toxic naturally-occurring substances. The oil is often used medicinally, but only after the ricin is removed through processing. If eaten raw, every part of the castor bean seed can be fatal. It is an ornamental woody shrub with star-shaped glossy green leaves and feathery flowers. It is native to Africa but was introduce to North America. It can be found in the Eastern and Southern parts of the US, often in disturbed areas.

Corn Cockle

This was originally found in Europe but became established in the US. It used to be used in herbal remedies, but its toxicity makes it dangerous to us. It is covered in fine hairs. Every stem had a single deep pink to purple flower and a ribbed bulb. It is a hardy plant and can be found in disturbed areas.

Daffodil

This flower may let you know that spring has arrived, but it is a common cause of poising, especially for pets. Eating any sections of this plant can create stomach problems. They can be found throughout North American in many different habitats.

Deadly Nightshade

This plant produces a cherry-like fruit that turns a shiny black color once ripe. The ground plant contains light-purple bell-shaped flowers and pale green leaves. It is pretty rare, but it can be found in the eastern and southern US.

Death Camas

Early settlers found out the hard way that this plant was deadly. Believing that it was onion or the edible camas plant, pioneers were surprised when they become ill after eating it. It has white, star-like flowers that are clustered around the end of a spike-like stem. Its leaves are long and grass-like and look like an onion plant. It is native to western North America and can be found in meadows.

Foxglove

Another European flower that found its way to the US, foxglove, can be spotted by its flowers that grow in a cluster around a long stem. The flower is funnel-shaped and typically points down. They come in a variety of colors. You can find its grey-green leaves near the base of the plant and can be a foot wide. Every part of the plant is poisonous.

Giant Hogweed

As you could guess by the name, the giant hogweed can reach 14 feet tall and five feet wide. It creates a white umbrella-shape flower cluster that can have up to 50 rays on each cluster. It has lobed leaves and measures up to five feet wide. Contact with the sap can cause burns and blisters. It can be found in Maine, New Hampshire, Vermont, Virginia, Michigan, Washington, Oregon, Maryland, Ohio, Pennsylvania, and New York.

Iris

You can easily spot an iris from the showy flowers that have three large sepals and three interior petals that droop down. All species are toxic, and the toxin is more concentrated in the roots. It can be found all over the US.

Jack-in-the-Pulpit

After you know what to look for, you won't be able to miss this flower. The flower will only be three to four inches tall with a tubular base and hood that curves over the tube. The hood will normally be green with purple and white stripes. It will have several big showy leaves. It can be found in moist woody areas in North America. It contains a calcium oxalate toxin that is mainly in its roots. You can touch, but don't consume it.

Jimson Weed

Also known as devil's snare is another nightshade plant that is well known for its various poisonous family members. It can grow between two to five feet with a thick stem and trumpet-shaped purple or white flowers. It has irregularly lobed leaves and is stinky when crushed. The seed pods are just as wicked with spikes on the outside. Every part is toxic and can cause hallucinations.

Larkspur

This plant is part of the buttercup family, but it isn't your regular buttercup. It grows in spikes and can reach five feet tall. It has a raceme of flowers that begin close to the base and extends to the top. It had a hollow stem, which distinguishes from monkshood, which is also poisonous. Every flower has a dolphin-like appearance. It is mainly found in the western and southern US. It likes moist soil.

Manchineel

The manchineel has been named the most dangerous tree in the world because of all of the toxins that are found in nearly every part of the tree. The sap can create blisters on the skin and can blind you if it gets into your eyes. A simple bit from its fruit can be fatal, and the smoke from burning leaves and branches can hurt your lung and eyes. This is a tropical tree and is native to Florida.

Monkshood

While monkshood is poisonous, it also has an unpleasant taste, so accidental poisoning is very rare. You can spot the plant by its distinctive purple or white flowers. They are arranged in a spike-like cluster with a hood shape that inspired its name. It can be found in mountainous areas.

Mountain Laurel

During the mid-summer, this can be found all over the Appalachian mountains. The flowers are showy with petals that are shaped like a bowl with distinct purple marks.

Oleander

This is a small, hardy shrub that has leather, slender, long leaves. When in bloom, it has a funnel-shaped flower and is commonly planted by the roadside. The flowers grow single or pairs and are typically bright in color. All parts of very toxic and should not be ingested. It can be found on the west coast and in southern states.

Poison Ivy and Oak

These, along with poison sumac, are the most common poisonous plants that everybody had heard of. It is most know for causing itching, swelling, and rash when it comes in contact with your skin. If you were to consume this, just imagine what your insides are going to feel like. Leaves of three are something you should remember to avoid coming in contact with poison ivy. The leaves are reddish in the spring, green in the summer, and yellow or orange in the fall. It can be found pretty much everywhere except for Hawaii and Alaska, and certain deserts.

Poison Sumac

Poison sumac looks different from the ivy and oak. It usually grows as a tree, five to 20 feet high, and likes swampy areas. It has a red stem and multiple leaves that have a smooth edge. It is most commonly found in the southern and eastern US.

Rosary Pea

These are native to India and were introduced to the US, where it is now seen as an invasive weed. It can be found in pastures, roadsides, abandoned farms, and other disturbed areas. They are highly toxic, and a single seed has the potential to kill you. It has a distinctive red and black pea that is uniform in size.

Water Hemlock

This is sometimes referred to as poison hemlock and is part of the same family as wild parsnip. It is not, however, related to the hemlock tree. It can easily be consumed with Queen Anne's lace and yarrow, which are edible. Water hemlock can be found throughout the US. The difference between this and Queen Anne's lace is that the stem is hairless, and they may contain a purplish splotch. On Queen Anne's lace, the stem is hairy, and it will often have a single dark purple flower in the middle of each umbel.

White Baneberry

This plant is hard to miss. It is white berries on a red stalk. It's a good thing that the berries look quite creepy because eating them can cause cardiac arrest. It is found in eastern North America.

White Hellebore

This plant is historically known for being poisonous, particularly in ancient Rome and Greece. Its cup-shaped flower with egg-shaped leaves is all toxic. The sap and seed can leave nasty chemical burns on the skin. It is native to Asia and Europe but is often planted in gardens in North America.

White Snakeroot

This is part of the Aster family, which includes daisies. It can grow to three feet tall with thin stems and egg-shaped leaves with a toothed edge and pointed tip. Their flowers are clustered with tiny, hairy protrusions. It can be found in the eastern part of North America, where it grows in wooded pastures and in forests. They contain tremetol, which is very poisonous.

Wild Parsnip

This is part of the parsley family that includes dill, celery, and carrot. It can grow up to five feet tall and will have yellow flowers that create an umbrella-shaped cluster. It can be found by the roadside, in pastures, and in fields. The sap of the wild parsnip causes the skin to become more sensitive to light. Most people don't realize when they have come in contact with wild parsnip until they break out in a blistering rash after being in the sun. It can be found throughout North America.

Wild Poinsettia

This is also called Fire on the Mountain; it has lobed leaves with irregular red blotches around the base of the topmost leaves. It has a milky sap that helps you identify it. It is toxic and irritating to the skin. They are native to tropical climates in South America, but it can be found in the southern part of the US. These are commonly seen around the holidays.

CHAPTER 6

The Basics Of Foraging

It is important that you understand the basics of ethical foraging when you make your first foraging trip. While we will go over most of what you will need to know, you can find more information in the book on foraging. Ethical foraging means that you won't ever take so much that you deplete the area of certain plants. This can prevent you from being able to return back to this area to forage the next year.

The responsible forager will always have conservation of the plants in mind when foraging. There are some plants that you won't have to worry about, but this will all depend on your state. Plus, there are some plants that are invasive, so it can be helpful to the environment to take as much as you can. With that in mind, let's take a look at some ways to make sure that you are foraging responsibly and ethically.

Make Sure You Can Be on the Land

This should be something people should naturally be conscious of, but sadly it's not. You should not forage for edible plants on private property unless you have the property owner's permission. When you ask for permission, you have to make sure that the property owner knows that you are going to respect their land, take only what you need, and offer them something in return.

When you are on public lands, like national or state forests and national parts, make sure that you check the rules of each place because the regulations can be very different. Some places will require that you get a permit, while others don't. Some may limit how much you can harvest. There are some parks where you can forage for berries, but you can for mushrooms. Always make sure you double-check and follow their rules when it comes to foraging.

Know How to Identify Plants and Forage Safely

The quickest way to get sick is to eat something you think is edible but isn't. You have to make sure that you know how to identify wild plants before harvesting them. This will ensure that you don't end up eating poisonous plants, but it is also important that you don't end up taking something that can't be used. You should never forage something unless you are 100% positive of what it is.

If you choose to do spore prints of mushrooms to help with identification, harvest just one of them before returning to harvest more once you find out what they are. It is always a good idea to leave something untouched and growing for sustainability.

Safety should always come first, no matter what. You should make sure that somebody else knows where you are going before you head out and when to expect you to be back. This will ensure somebody will know to come looking for you should you get lost. Make sure you are dressed for the occasion as well, and that you have the right equipment with you.

Remember the Four Rs

The four Rs are roadways, right of ways, residences, and railroads. Most experienced foragers will tell you to avoid busy roads, right of ways, railroads, and any built-up areas because the edibles in these spaces may end up being contaminated by herbicides, particulates, fertilizers, and so on. But then there are some who believe that it all depends on what foods you are looking for. Generally speaking, plants adapt to the environment that they are in through their roots and leaves. This means the fruits, as long as they are at a distance from the ground, are typically fit and safe to consume. No matter what you are gathering, though, make sure that you use your common sense. If something arouses your suspicion or it seems to be contaminated, don't eat it.

Know Your Protect Species

Protected species lists will change all the time. To make sure that you don't hurt the environment or accrue costly fines, talk to a local expert about protected species before you head out foraging. However, if a plant has been labeled protected, then it is rare and nearly impossible to find. This means it is probably very unlikely for a forager, expert or novice, to be able to find decent amounts of any protected plant that is on the cusp of going extinct.

Don't Take the Only Plant

Follow the rule of abundance. If you can only find one plant is a sizable area, leave it untouched. You should never take the only edible plant of a wild species as it will likely be unable to regenerate. Remember that the planet, forest, and animals need that single specimen more so than you do. Similar to this idea, never take everything from a single spot. You should only remove less than 10% of any one plant.

Take Only What You Need

Forage only what you are going to need to make whatever you have in mind. Only take enough leaves to dry them out for the winter's tea drinking. Leave all of the others for the earth. You don't need to hoard more than your home is going to need.

Harvest Your Plants Wisely

You should harvest from plants that look like they have been stressed from fire, flooding, drought, or any other situation. Take only from healthy plants that are abundantly available. When you take part of the plant, harvest just the top 2/3's of the plant, leaving all the rest for it to regenerate and spread as nature would like it to. If you need the plant's roots, dig it up carefully and cut off parts of it with a knife instead of just ripping out of the earth. When you take responsible care during harvest, it will help to make sure the plant stays healthy.

As you make your way out into the world looking for wild edible plants, enjoy the beauty of nature. Allow the different plants to show themselves to you. When finding these edible plants, follow the steps that we have discussed to keep your foraging fun and safe for you and the earth.

CHAPTER 7

Recipes For Edible Wild Plants

Buffalo Milkweed Pods

You'll Need:

- Favorite hot wing sauce
- Water, .5 c
- Almond milk, .5 c
- Egg

- Turmeric, cayenne, oregano, and paprika, 1 tsp each
- Garlic powder, 1 tbsp
- Flour, .25 c
- Panko, 1.5 c
- Milkweed pods

You'll Do:

1. Start by getting your oven to 350.
2. Combine all of your dry ingredients together. Beat together the water, almond milk, and egg together and then mix it into the dry ingredients. Combine well.
3. Dip the milkweed pods into the batter and then lay them out on a baking sheet that has been lined with parchment. Let them bake for 15 to 20 minutes.
4. Once they are crisp, move them to a bowl. Pour in your favorite wing sauce and make sure that they are well coated. Spread them back out on the baking sheet and cook them for another ten minutes. Enjoy.

Cattail Rice

You'll Need:

- Pepper, 1 tsp
- Vegetable broth, 2 c
- Garlic salt, .5 tsp
- Uncooked rice, 1 c
- Diced onion
- Chopped young cattail shoots, 1 c
- Butter, 2 tbsp + 1 tbsp

You'll Do:

1. Start by adding the two tablespoons of butter to a pan and letting it melt. Add in the cattail shoots and cook until they are soft. This will take about five to ten minutes. If you need to, you can add in the extra better. Once soft, turn the heat down to low and add in the onions, pepper, and garlic, cooking until translucent.
2. As your veggies are cooking, cook your rice according to the package directions. If you need to, adjust the rice to water ratio according to the directions.
3. After the rice has been cooked, mix in the cooked vegetables. Cover the pot and let everything sit for two to three minutes. Enjoy.

Dandy Pasta

You'll Need:

- Favorite spice mixture, 2 tbsp
- Coconut oil, 3 tbsp
- Butter, .25 c
- Garlic, 2 cloves
- Red onion
- Dandelions with roots, 2 to 3 c
- Bowtie pasta, 2 c

You'll Do:

1. Start by cutting the roots off of the leaves right at the top so that the leaves will stay together. Finely chop up the roots along with the garlic and onion.
2. As this cooks, follow the directions on the packaging for your pasta and cook the pasta until done.
3. Melt your butter in a pan along with the coconut oil. Add in the spices and mix well. Add the dandelion root, onion, and garlic, and let this cook for five to ten minutes.
4. After it is done cooking, add in the cooked pasta and stir everything together. Let this simmer together for one to two minutes. Mix in the dandelion leaves. Let it simmer for a minute and enjoy.

Garlic Mustard Stuffed Mushrooms

You'll Need:

- Melted butter, 1 tbsp
- Grated cheese, 1.5 c
- Finely chopped onion
- Finely chopped lambs quarters, .75 c
- Finely chopped garlic mustard, 1 c
- Cream cheese, 4 oz
- White mushrooms, 20

You'll Do:

1. Start by getting your oven to 350.
2. Wash the mushrooms and get rid of the stems. Hollow out the insides of the mushrooms to make space for the filling. Cover your mushrooms as you work on the filling so that they don't dry out.
3. Add the onions, both greens, and cream cheese to a bowl and mix them together. Make sure that everything is well combined.
4. Brush the mushrooms with your melted butter. Next, spoon the filling into each of the mushrooms.
5. Lay some parchment out onto a baking sheet and place the mushrooms out on it. Sprinkle the tops with your favorite grated cheese.
6. Bake them for about 20 minutes. Broil them to crisp up the cheese and enjoy.

Kale, Lambs Quarters, and Cheese Manicotti

You'll Need:

- Parsley
- Pepper and salt
- Grated parmesan, .5 c
- Mozzarella, 1.5 c – divided
- Beaten eggs, 2
- Ricotta cheese, 18 oz
- Finely chopped kale, 1 c
- Finely chopped lamb's quarters, 1 c
- Spaghetti sauce, 2 to 3 c
- Cooked manicotti shells, 1 box

You'll Do:

1. Start by mixing together the kale, lamb's quarters, ricotta, egg, parmesan, pepper, salt, and 1 cup of mozzarella.
2. Carefully fill each of the cooked manicotti shells with the filling.
3. In a casserole dish, evenly spread a layer of spaghetti sauce over the bottom. Lay the stuffed manicotti on top of the sauce. Make sure that you don't lay one manicotti on top of another.

4. Spread the rest of the spaghetti sauce over the shells and then sprinkle on the rest of the mozzarella cheese.

5. Once your oven is at 350, bake for 30 minutes.

6. Allow this to cool for about five minutes and then serve. Garnish with some parsley if desired.

Purslane Egg Cups

You'll Need:

- Favorite spices
- Cheddar cheese, .25 c
- Eggs, 12
- Milk, .25 c
- Finely chopped onions, 2
- Small pepper, chopped
- Chopped purslane, 2 c

You'll Do:

1. Start by making sure your oven is at 350. Take a muffin pan and grease it well.
2. In a pan with some butter, add the pepper and onion and sauté for about five minutes.
3. Using a food processor or blender, add the spices of your choosing, milk, eggs, and cheese. One the pepper and onions are cooked, add those in as well. Blend everything together.
4. Pour into a bowl and stir in the purslane and any other wild greens you would like to use.
5. Divide the egg mixture between the cups in the muffin pan and bake for 20 to 25 minutes, or until the eggs are completely cooked.

Stuffed Milkweed Pods

You'll Need:

- Bread crumbs
- Boiled and split milkweed pots, 20
- Pepper and salt
- Chopped jalapeno
- Cooked bacon, 2 slices
- Diced red onion, 1 tbsp
- Softened cream cheese, 4 oz

You'll Do:

1. Start by setting your oven to 375.
2. Place the cream cheese in a bowl with the pepper, salt, bacon, jalapeno, and onion. Mix everything together until well combined.
3. Go through the boiled milkweed pods and get rid of any immature seeds and silk from them. Spoon in about two teaspoons of the cream cheese mixture, filling the pod until full.
4. Roll the seam of filling into the bread crumbs and then sit them seam side up on a parchment-lined baking sheet.
5. Bake them for 15 to 20 minutes.

Weed Burgers

You'll Need:

- Favorite spices, 1 tbsp
- Finely chopped wild edibles of choice, 1 c
- Breadcrumbs, .75 c
- Finely chopped onion
- Chopped garlic, 3 cloves
- Salt, .5 tsp
- Beaten eggs, 4
- Cooked quinoa, 2.66 c

You'll Do:

1. Start by mixing together the spices, salt, eggs, and quinoa. Mix in the garlic and onion. Lastly, stir in the wild edibles and breadcrumbs. Allow this mixture to rest for a few minutes so that the breadcrumbs can absorb the moisture.
2. Form into patties and fry them in a pan for about five minutes on each side.
3. You can enjoy the burgers on buns just like you would a regular burger.

Wild Potato Pancakes

You'll Need:

- Pepper, 1 tsp
- Salt, 1 tsp
- Garlic powder, 2 tsp
- Flour, 2 tbsp
- Hemp seeds, 2 tbsp
- Chopped mushrooms, .25 c
- Chopped wild greens, .5 c
- Chopped onions, .33 c
- Eggs, 2
- Grated potatoes, 4 c

You'll Do:

1. Start by melting some butter in a pan. Add the onions and sauté for a couple of minutes and then mix in the mushrooms. Cook for another two minutes and set it off of the heat.
2. In a bowl, add the spices, flour, seeds, eggs, sautéed vegetables, and grated potatoes. Mix everything together for about three minutes to make sure everything is well combined.

3. In a frying pan, melt a bit of butter to make sure the pancakes don't stick. With your hands, create balls from the batter. As you do this, you will notice that the potatoes contain some liquid. Squeeze out some of this liquid.

4. Lay the ball onto the frying pan and flatten it with a spatula to about a half-inch thick. Cook until both sides are golden brown. Add extra butter if you need to so that they don't stick.

5. Continue until all of the batter is used and enjoy.

Wild Roasted Cabbage

You'll Need:

- Crumbled cooked bacon, 5 slices – if desired
- Grated cheese – if desired
- Pepper and salt
- Ground dried stinging nettle, to taste
- Chopped garlic, to taste
- Chopped onion, to taste
- Chopped garlic mustard, to taste
- Olive oil, 4 to 6 tbsp
- Head of cabbage

You'll Do:

1. Start by getting your oven to 350.
2. Lay the cabbage on a chopping board and slice into ¼ inch thick slices. Do your best to hold the leaves together. You can usually get four to six slices.
3. Brush the bottom of the slices with oil and then lay them on a parchment-lined baking sheet.
4. Add the rest of the oil to a bowl and combine with the garlic, pepper, salt, and nettle. Brush this on top of the cabbage slices.

5. Sprinkle the tops of the cabbage with the onions and garlic mustard.

6. Bake this for 20 minutes. Take out and top with the cheese and bacon if you are using them. Let this back for about 15 minutes more. Enjoy.

Buttered Chickweed

You'll Need:

- Pepper
- Salt
- Butter
- Finely chopped onion
- Chopped chickweed, 2 c

You'll Do:

1. Start by washing the chickweed. Bring a pot of salted water to a boil and add the chickweed into the water. Let this cook for a couple of minutes and then drain well.
2. Add some butter to a pan. Add in the onion and sauté until translucent. Add in the chickweed. Season with some pepper and salt or any other spices that you would like.

Plantain Salad

You'll Need:

- Salt, 1 tsp
- Wine vinegar, 1/8 c
- Olive oil, 1/8 c
- Chopped garlic, 1 to 2 cloves
- Finely chopped celery stalk
- Thinly chopped onion
- Can of drained chickpeas
- Finely chopped cabbage, .5 c
- Chopped plantain, 2 c

You'll Do:

1. Start by mixing all of the above ingredients together, except for the vinegar and oil. Place the in the refrigerator. Once this has chilled well, add in the vinegar and oil.
2. If you find that the salad is a bit on the dry side, you can add some more vinegar and olive oil. Taste and adjust any seasonings that you need to.

Blueberry Labrador Tea

You'll Need:

- Lemon juice, 1 tbsp – if desired
- Water, 1 c
- Blueberries, 1.5 c
- Labrador tea, 4 c

You'll Do:

1. Add the blueberries and water to a pot and let them come to a boil. Turn the heat down and simmer, stirring often, until the blueberries start to break down. This will take about five to ten minutes. Add the blueberries into the brewed tea. Add in your favorite sweetener, stir, and then let it come to room temperature.
2. Place in the fridge until cold, usually about two hours. Strain the mixture into a pitcher and mix in the lemon juice.

Burdock Tonic Tea

You'll Need:

- Dried peppermint leaves, to taste
- Dried red clover flowers, 2
- Dried dandelion root, 1 tsp
- Dried burdock root, 1 tsp

You'll Do:

1. Start by mixing all of the ingredients together and then place them into a large mug.
2. Pour in some boiling water, cover the cup, and let it steep for 30 minutes. Strain and enjoy.

Healthy Heart Tea

You'll Need:

- Cold water, 5 c
- Fennel seeds, 2 pinches
- Ginger root, 2 slices
- Hawthorn berries, 1/8 c
- Motherwort, 1 tsp

You'll Do:

1. Pour the water into a pot and add in all of the herbs. Let this come to a boil, turn the heat down, and simmer for 20 minutes.
2. Let it cool enough to drink, and add in lemon or honey if you want. Enjoy.

Highbush Cranberry Juice

You'll Need:

- Maple syrup, 1 tsp
- Orange juice, 2 c
- Highbush cranberries, 2 c
- Water, 3 c

You'll Do:

1. Start by adding the water to a pot and letting it come up to a boil. Turn off the heat. Add the berries to the water and mash them a bit. Allow this to sit for 30 minutes.
2. Strain the water and allow the liquid to cool. Once cool, add in the syrup and orange juice. This will keep in the fridge for five days.

Immune Boosting Coffee

You'll Need:

- Pinch of salt
- Water, 4 c
- Coffee, .5 c
- Powdered turkey tails, 1 tbsp
- Powdered tinder conk, 1 tbsp
- Powdered chaga, 1 tbsp

You'll Do:

1. Start by adding the water to your drip coffee maker. Place the turkey tail, tinder conk, and chaga into the filter and then add the coffee on top of them. Add in a pinch of salt to help with the bitterness.
2. Brew as you normally work, and sweeten if desired.

Fennel and Angelica Cookies

You'll Need:

- Flour, 2.5 c
- Fennel seeds, 1 tbsp
- Chopped angelica leaves, 2 tbsp
- Light beaten egg yolk
- Sugar, .5 to .75 c
- Butter, 1 c

You'll Do:

1. Start by adding the butter and sugar to a bowl and mix well. Stir in the angelica and egg yolk. Slowly add in the flour and fennel. Stir everything together so that it is well combined.
2. Once blended, cover, and refrigeration for 30 minutes.
3. Get your oven to 375 and place some parchment paper on some baking sheets.
4. Take the dough out and roll golf ball sizes of dough between your hands. Flatten them out on the parchment to eighth of an inch thick. You can also roll the dough out and use cookie cutters if you would prefer.
5. Bake for 12 to 15 minutes. Let them cool for ten minutes and then place them on a wire rack to cool completely.

Bee Balm Cookies

You'll Need:

- Orange zest, 4 tsp
- Chopped bee balm flowers and leaves, 4 to 5 tbsp
- Flour, 1 c
- Powdered sugar, .5 c
- Butter, .5 c

You'll Do:

1. Start by beating the butter with the bee balm, sugar, and orange zest until well combined. Add in the flour and mix together. You may have to use your hands to really get it mixed together because it will get thick. Make sure you don't overwork the dough once you add the flour. Once smooth, roll into a cylinder and wrap in parchment. Chill for two hours.
2. Once chilled, slice the dough into quarter-inch slices. Place them on a baking sheet about an inch apart.
3. Bake for eight to ten minutes at 350. Enjoy.

Coltsfoot Sorbet

You'll Need:

- Coltsfood flowers, .5 c
- Sugar, .25 c
- Water, 2 c

You'll Do:

1. Start by adding the water and sugar to a pot. Stir until the sugar has dissolved.
2. Add in the coltsfoot and let it come up to a boil. Turn the heat down and cook for five minutes. Set this off of the heat and let it cool.
3. Pour into your ice cream maker and fix it according to the directions. You can enjoy this now or place it in the freezer for later.

Dandelion Banana Bread

You'll Need:

- Baking soda, .5 tsp
- Baking powder, 1 tsp
- Dandelion flower petals, .33 c
- Flour, 1.25 c
- Brown sugar, .33 c
- Egg
- Olive oil, .5 c
- Ripe banana

You'll Do:

1. Start by mashing up the banana and mixing in the sugar, egg, and oil. Stir in the baking soda, baking powder, dandelion flowers, and flour. Mix until everything comes together. If you want, you can also add chocolate chips or walnuts.
2. Scoop into a greased loaf pan.
3. Bake for 20 to 25 minutes at 350.
4. Once cooked through, slice and enjoy.

Honey Cattail Cookies

You'll Need:

- Coconut butter, 4 tbsp
- Honey, .5 c
- Cinnamon, 3 tsp
- Vanilla, 1 tsp
- Oats, 2 c
- Coconut flakes, 2 c
- A brown cattail

You'll Do:

1. Start by grinding the cattail fluff up with the oats to create fluffy flour. Add this to a bowl along with the remaining ingredients. Knead until thoroughly mixed and then form into cookies.
2. You can eat this raw, or you can place them in the oven for one to two hours at the lowest setting. Enjoy.

Nutty Plantain Snack

You'll Need:

- Sea salt
- Olive oil
- Sesame seeds, 3 handfuls
- Pumpkin seeds, 3 handfuls
- Plantain seeds, 1 handful

You'll Do:

1. Start by adding all of the seeds into a bowl. Add in the salt and olive oil, making sure that the seeds are coated well in the oil. You can also add in other spices if you would like to.
2. Spread this out on a baking sheet and roast for ten to 15 minutes at 250.
3. Let them cool and enjoy.

Pine Cookies

You'll Need:

- Vanilla, 1 tsp
- Eggs, 3
- Melted butter, .5 c
- Red or white pine powder, 8 tbsp
- Sugar, 1.5 c
- Flour, 3 c

You'll Do:

1. Start by adding the dry ingredients into a bowl.
2. In a separate bowl, mix together the vanilla, eggs, and butter. Stir the wet ingredients into the dry ones until well combined.
3. Roll the dough into balls and lay them on a cookie sheet. Using a fork, press the cookies out to a quarter-inch thick.
4. Bake them for ten to 12 minutes at 325. Enjoy.

Pine Rum Balls

You'll Need:

- Shredded coconut, 2 tbsp
- Ground up pine needles, 2 tbsp
- Rum, 2 tbsp
- Half of a pine cake, crumbled

You'll Do:

1. Start by breaking up the pine cake into small pieces. Add in the rum, slowly, until you can start forming the cake into balls. If you need to, you can add in a bit more rum.
2. In a different bowl, combine the coconut and pine.
3. Roll the cake balls into the coconut and pin mixture. You can also use powdered sugar and chocolate sprinkles if you would prefer.
4. Place them on a plate to chill in the fridge for two hours. Serve and enjoy.

CONCLUSION

Thank you for making it through to the end of the book, let's hope it was informative and able to provide you with all of the tools you need to achieve your goals whatever they may be.

The next step is to start exploring the world of edible wild plants. While it may sound like a hard thing to start doing, foraging for your own food can be a rewarding experience. You don't have to replace your entire diet with foraged foods. Just trying some of the edible wild foods will make a difference, and you will start to realize it's not as hard as it may have originally seemed.

The most important thing to remember is to be nice to the planet when you are foraging. Don't just ravage an area because you find a lot of good food. Take only what you are going to use and make sure that the plants will be able to replenish themselves before you return to that spot again. Be ethical in your foraging.

Also, never go foraging blind, especially while you are still new at it. Make sure you have something with you that can help you identify plants. Better yet, take a trip through an area that you would like to forage in and just study the plants to figure out what you've got. Once you have identified some safe plants, you can come back at a later time and forage. The last thing you want to do is assume that something is safe because it "kind of looks like it" and then get sick, or worse, once you eat it.

Lastly, remember that a lot of these edible wild plants can also be used to treat various ailments. Our ancestors only had plants to cure health problems. It's even believed that for every disease mankind suffers from, there is a plant that can cure it. Unfortunately, modern medicine has made it seem like plants can't help treat ailments. I'm not telling you that herbs and plants should be used in place of modern medicine, it shouldn't, but you can tap into the power of plants from time to time to help supplement your doctor's treatment. If you feel like you have a serious ailment, always seek a doctor's opinion first.

Above all else, enjoy the foraging process. Commune with nature and learn something from her.

Finally, if you found this book useful in any way, a review on Amazon is always appreciated!